A Mensa Book of Logic Puzzles

LOGIC is a method of reasoning that involves a series of statements, each of which must be true if the statement that comes before it is true. Logic requires no prior knowledge, no mathematical or linguistic skills — just the ability to think logically.

A MENSA BOOK OF LOGIC PUZZLES tests your ability to think logically. The puzzles, graded from easy to very difficult, provide an opportunity to match your logic-ability with the best in the world. A 'Hints' section is provided to start you off if you get stuck. The spatial and sequential patterns of these puzzles will stimulate both your intellect and your imagination. Answers are given at the back of the book and where necessary, explained!

And remember, all puzzles in this book are presented by a Mensa member — the high IQ international society.

About Mensa

Mensa is more than just puzzles. Contrary as this may seem to the popular opinion that Mensa is a group of intelligent people who set and solve puzzles, Mensa is an international society of the some of the most intelligent people in the world. Founded in Oxford in England in 1946 it today has a worldwide membership of 110,000 in 110 countries and with 28 national chapters operating around the world, including India.

The only qualification for membership of Mensa is a score that is within the upper two per cent of the general population, measured on an approved, supervised intelligence test. This test is the only way to get Mensa membership.

Mensa is a Latin word meaning 'table', implying a round table society where every member is equal. Mensa's policy is to include intelligent people of every opinion and background. It is open to all who meet the intelligence criterion. You too may be a potential member. And if you decide to apply for Mensa membership, we wish you all success.

A
MENSA
BOOK OF
LOGIC
PUZZLES

•

ALAN WAREHAM

Orient
Paperbacks
DELHI | MUMBAI | HYDERABAD

To Tracey

Acknowledgements

I wish to thank the British Mensa Committee, under the chairmanship of Sir Clive Sinclair, for allowing the use of the name Mensa on the front cover of this book. Thanks also to British Mensa's Executive Director, Harold Gale, for his assistance with my application and to Ken Russell, Puzzle Editor of Mensa, for his help and advice. Last, but not least, a special thank you to my wife Tracey, not just for her help in checking the puzzles but for her everlasting support and enthusiasm.

ISBN : 978-81-222-0148-2

A Mensa Book of Logic Puzzles

Subject: Puzzles / Mental Skills

© Alan Wareham

1st Published 1993
6th Printing 2013

Published in arrangement with
Cassell plc., England

Published by
Orient Paperbacks
(A division of Vision Books Pvt. Ltd.)
5A/8 Ansari Road, New Delhi-110 002
www.orientpaperbacks.com

Printed at
Anand Sons, Delhi-110 092, India

Cover Printed at
Ravindra Printing Press, Delhi-110 006, India

Contents

Introduction

Tests of logical reasoning are an integral part of intelligence tests conducted by Mensa. They are similar to the puzzles in this book in that they are 'culture free'. No general knowledge or mathematical ability is necessary to solve any of the puzzles in this book, only the ability to think logically. The puzzles have been graded as follows :

    * Average
   ** Challenging
  *** Difficult

Don't be put off by the sight of a 'difficult' or a 'challenging' puzzle. The puzzles have been grouped so that puzzles of a similar type begin with the average type of puzzle, and progress to more difficult examples. Interspersed amongst the similar types of puzzles are 'one-off' logic puzzles which are completely different to any other puzzle in the book. These have also been graded, but are not arranged in order of difficulty.

Before the full solutions at the end of the book there is a 'Hints' section. Half of the puzzles in the book have a letter H followed by a number, next to the title. This indicates that there is a hint given in the 'Hints' section to give you a start on solving the puzzle, rather than having to look at the answer immediately if you get stuck. There are only nine different hints, but some hints apply to more than one type of puzzle. The puzzles for which there is no hint given are either 'one-offs' where a hint would spoil the puzzle, or puzzles for which, if any sort of hint were given, too much of the answer would be revealed.

The puzzles have also been cross-referenced with two numbers, a question number (Q) and an answer number (A). This has been done so as to mix up the order of the answers, thereby avoiding the risk, when consulting them, of seeing the answer to the next puzzle before attempting to solve it.

Alan Wareham

Logic Puzzles

Q1   Paint-by-Numbers*   A31
Shown below is a 'Modern Art' paint-by-numbers grid.
You only have four different colours and must not paint two
adjoining sections, including the border, the same colour.
Which two of the twelve numbered sections will be the
same colour as the border?

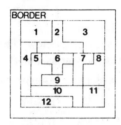

Q2   Who's Who?*   A42
Harry and Fred are called Smith and Jones, but I'm not
sure if it's Harry Smith and Fred Jones or Harry Jones and
Fred Smith. Given that two of the following statements are
false, what is Harry's surname?

1. Harry's surname is Jones.
2. Harry's surname is Smith.
3. Fred's surname is Smith.

Q3   Card Sharp*   A63
Row 1 = Four cards with different letters on both sides.
Row 2 = The same four cards from Row 1, two of which
         have been turned over, all four of which are in
         different positions.
Row 3 = The same four cards from Row 2, two more of

which have been turned over, and all four of which are again in different positions to the positions they were in in Rows 1 and 2.

Which letter is on the other side of each of the four cards in Row 3?

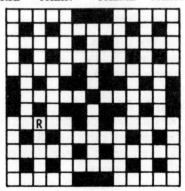

Q4   Grid Fill**   H1, A11

Fit the 36 words into the grid below. The letter R has been entered into the grid for you as a start.

ADORN	AMPLE	AORTA	ARROW	BESET	BLAME
CLAMP	DALLY	DAZED	ELDER	EPOCH	EXACT
FILET	GALEA	HALVE	HAZEL	INDUE	IRATE
JAUNT	JOINT	MADAM	OCTAL	OPERA	REDID
REFER	RIDGE	RODEO	ROYAL	SEPIA	SPRAT
SURGE	TERSE	THEIR	THEME	TREAT	UNDER

Q5 Every Which Way* A72

There are two different ways of completing a 4 × 4 grid so that all four columns, rows and both diagonals contain the numbers 1, 2, 3 and 4, and the top row contains the numbers in ascending order. What are they?

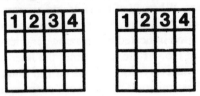

Q6 Flipover** H3, A107

Diagram One is that of the numbers 1, 2, 3 and 4; each of which is surrounded by eight circles, all of which contain a different letter. The eight circles around each of the four numbers can be 'flipped over' the number itself either vertically or horizontally. For example, in diagram One, if the letters around the number 1 were flipped vertically, A and F would swap places, B and G would swap places, C and H would swap places and D and E would remain in the same position.

Diagram Two is that of Diagram One after each of the four numbers have been flipped over either vertically or horizontally. In which direction have the letters around each number been flipped over to arrive at the positions shown in diagram Two?

Diagram One　Ⓐ Ⓓ Ⓕ Ⓘ Ⓚ Ⓝ Ⓟ Ⓢ Ⓤ
　　　　　　　Ⓑ ① Ⓖ ② Ⓛ ③ Ⓠ ④ Ⓥ
　　　　　　　Ⓒ Ⓔ Ⓗ Ⓙ Ⓜ Ⓞ Ⓡ Ⓣ Ⓦ

Diagram Two　Ⓕ Ⓓ Ⓒ Ⓙ Ⓚ Ⓞ Ⓤ Ⓢ Ⓡ
　　　　　　　Ⓖ ① Ⓑ ② Ⓛ ③ Ⓥ ④ Ⓠ
　　　　　　　Ⓗ Ⓔ Ⓐ Ⓘ Ⓜ Ⓝ Ⓦ Ⓣ Ⓟ

Q7 Laser Maze** H2, A83

The diagram below represents an aerial view of a room which has been divided into 100 squares, as shown by the dotted lines. In each of the squares there should be a dot marked on the floor in the centre of the square, or a double-sided mirror. When all of the dots and mirrors are in their correct places, a laser beam can enter the room at square A1 in the direction indicated by an arrow, and leave the room from square J10. At the same time, the laser beam shines over each and every dot marked on the floor. When the beam reaches a mirror it 'bounces off' at an angle of 90°, but it never crosses itself. If the beam hits the outside wall it is absorbed by the wall and can go no further.

Fourteen of the dots/mirrors are not in place: five dots (X), six mirrors from lower left to upper right (Y), and three mirrors from upper left to lower right (Z). See if you can determine which of the squares containing '?' should be replaced by:

1. X squares;   2. Y squares;   3. Z squares.

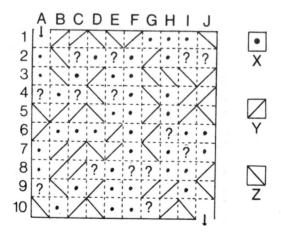

Q8   Stationary Stationery*   H4, A93

The other day, the stationery clerk asked George, Fred and Arthur if they would carry some parcels of stationery to the typists' office. There were six parcels in all: one large parcel, which weighed the same as the two medium-sized parcels, which in turn weighed the same as the three small parcels. The stationery clerk then said that one person could carry the large parcel, one person could carry the two medium-sized parcels and one person could carry the three small parcels; that way all three would be carrying the same weight of stationery. George, Fred and Arthur weren't very happy about having to carry the stationery anyway and said that they would only carry the stationery to the typists on the following conditions.

George would only carry the two medium-sized parcels if Fred carried the three small parcels. Fred would only carry the three small parcels if George carried the large parcel. George would only carry the large parcel if Arthur carried the two medium-sized parcels. Arther would only carry the two medium-sized parcels if Fred carried the large parcel. George would only carry the three small parcels if Arthur carried the large parcel. All this time the stationery remained stationary. Eventually the stationery clerk came up with a solution to keep all three happy. Who carried what to the typists?

Q9 Letter Boxes* H5, A118

When the diagram below is complete, each column and row should contain the letters A, B, C, D, E, F, G, H, I and J. See if you can complete the diagram by fitting the nine blocks of nine letters into the nine highlighted squares, then filling in the spaces along the top row and in the first column.

	F		J		B		
E							
A							
H							

D	I	B
J	H	F
A	F	J

J	E	H
C	D	G
E	G	I

C	A	D
F	J	H
I	D	E

C	G	A
B	A	I
D	H	C

B	H	F
D	.	E
G	F	A

B	C	G
H	E	C
E	G	I

H	A	D
A	B	J
F	C	B

J	E	G
G	C	B
H	B	J

F	I	E
I	D	F
A	J	D

Q10 Logic Box* H6, A21

Using the following clues, place the letters A to I inclusive into the grid. G is above I and to the right of B. C is to the right of H and above I which is to the left of D. B is to the left of E. H is above F and B. A is above E. ('Above' refers to two letters in the same column. 'Left of/right of' refers to two letters in the same row.)

12

QII What Next?* A128
Find the next most appropriate square:

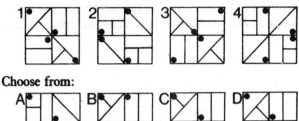

Choose from:

QI2 Blocked** H7, A138
Each of the 25 blocks of four letters shown below can be rotated about its centre, either 90° clockwise or 90° anti-clockwise. When all of the 25 blocks are in their correct positions, all ten rows and columns contain the letters A to J only once.

Twelve of the blocks shown below are not in their correct positions. Six blocks have been rotated clockwise and six blocks have been rotated anticlockwise. Given that at least two blocks, and no more than three blocks, have been rotated in each of the five rows and columns of blocks, which 12 of the 25 have been rotated and in which direction?

	A	B	C	D	E
1	C A / D E	D F / F J	G H / B C	I B / H I	G J / A E
2	I C / E B	H I / A G	J B / H D	G D / F A	F C / E J
3	J D / F H	B G / D A	A J / F C	E G / C E	H I / I B
4	A G / J F	C J / I B	E F / I E	D B / H C	D A / G H
5	I B / H G	E H / C E	A G / D I	F J / J A	C D / B F

13

Q13 Square Cut* A52

Divide the diagram into four parts of equal size and shape, each part of which must contain the numbers 1, 2, 3 and 4. The four parts should then be rearranged to form a square.

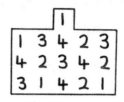

Q1 Wordsquare* A143

Fit the 12 blocks into the grid to form a wordsquare which reads the same down and across.

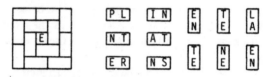

Q15 Odd One Out* A1

Which of the six cubes shown cannot be constructed from the flattened cube below?

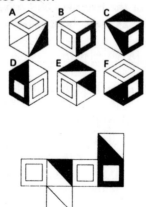

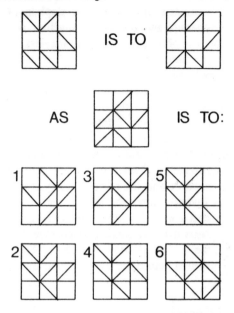

Q17   The History of Invention★   H8, A129

I had a list of various inventions which were in date order, but the piece of paper on which they were listed was torn in half, one half of which has been lost. Given the list of years in which the inventions were invented and the information below, see if you can match all of the inventions with the year in which they were invented.

This is the half I have left, on which is written the years of invention:

> 1320, 1607, 1710, 1721, 1763, 1764, 1783, 1815, 1841,
> 1856, 1868, 1876, 1877, 1898, 1899, 1935, 1939, 1941.

Gunpowder, the telescope, pianoforte and the mercury thermometer were all invented before the spinning jenny, the steam engine and the hot air balloon. Steel, the wireless and the sewing machine were all invented before radar and the tank. The miner's safety lamp, the telephone, gunpowder, steel, dynamite and the sewing machine were all invented before the phonograph and the wireless, the two of which, and the tank, were invented before radar, the jet engine and polyester.

Gunpowder, the spinning jenny, the steam engine, the mercury thermometer and the hot air balloon were all invented before the miner's safety lamp and the sewing machine. Polyester was invented after dynamite, radar and the jet engine. The pianoforte was invented after the telescope and gunpowder. Dynamite was invented after steel, the sewing machine and the miner's safety lamp.

Steel was invented after the sewing machine which in turn was invented after the miner's safety lamp. The wireless was invented after the phonograph, the jet engine after radar, and the telephone after dynamite. The spinning jenny was invented before the steam engine and the hot air balloon.

Q18   Odd Block Out*   A37
Which is the odd block out?

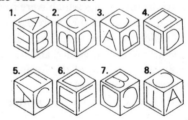

Q19   Done What?*   A108
Dave said Bill did it, Bill said Arthur did it, Arthur said Eddie did it, Eddie said Charlie did it and Charlie said that he didn't do it. If Charlie didn't do it, one of the five of them did do it and only one of them is telling the truth; who did do it?

Q20 Number Fill★ A73

Given that the same number does not appear in two adjacent squares, either vertically, horizontally or diagonally, fit the numbers 1 to 9 inclusive four times each into the 6 × 6 grid. Only one number should be entered into each of the 36 squares. The numbers appear next to the row and beneath the column into which they should be placed.

```
          1 3 4 5 7 9
          1 2 3 8 8 9
          2 3 4 4 6 6
          1 5 5 7 7 8
          1 2 2 6 9 9
          3 4 5 6 7 8

   2  1  2  2  1  1
   5  1  3  5  2  3
   5  3  7  6  4  3
   5  4  7  6  4  6
   9  8  7  9  4  6
   9  8  8  9  8  7
```

Q21 Where Do They Live?★ A148

There are five houses in a street, numbered 1, 2, 3, 4 and 5, each with one resident. Given the seven lists of five surnames and the house in which each of them resides, see if you can determine the surname of the five residents and the number of the house in which each resides. There is a catch, as you may have noticed already: not all seven lists are the same, therefore they cannot all be correct. In fact none of the lists are completely correct. The number at the bottom of each list is the number of resident(s) whose surnames have been listed next to the correct house number.

House no.	A	B	C	D	E	F	G
1	Brown	Smith	Allen	Smith	Brown	Duffy	Duffy
2	Sharma	Johnson	Dodds	Dodds	Sharma	Dodds	Johnson
3	Anderson	Russell	Finlay	Anderson	Finlay	Williams	Williams
4	Carter	Morris	Krishnan	Morris	Morris	Arthur	Parker
5	McDonald	Singh	Humphries	Grant	Grant	Singh	Scott
	(Two)	(Two)	(One)	(One)	(One)	(One)	(One)

17

Q22 Flipover** H3, A119

Diagram One is that of the numbers 1, 2, 3 and 4, each of which is surrounded by eight circles, all of which contain a different letter. The eight circles around each of the four numbers can be 'flipped over' the number itself either vertically or horizontally. For example, in Diagram One, if the letters around the number 1 were flipped vertically, A and F would swap places, B and G would swap places, C and H would swap places and D and E would remain in the same position.

Diagram Two is that of Diagram One after the four numbers have been flipped over a total of six times. Each number has been flipped over at least once but no more than twice. In what order, and in which direction, have the letters around each number been flipped over to arrive at the positions shown in Diagram Two?

Diagram One

Ⓐ Ⓓ Ⓕ Ⓘ Ⓚ Ⓝ Ⓟ Ⓢ Ⓤ
Ⓑ ① Ⓖ ② Ⓛ ③ Ⓠ ④ Ⓥ
Ⓒ Ⓔ Ⓗ Ⓙ Ⓜ Ⓞ Ⓡ Ⓣ Ⓦ

Diagram Two

Ⓒ Ⓔ Ⓜ Ⓙ Ⓡ Ⓞ Ⓕ Ⓣ Ⓦ
Ⓑ ① Ⓛ ② Ⓠ ③ Ⓖ ④ Ⓥ
Ⓐ Ⓓ Ⓚ Ⓘ Ⓟ Ⓝ Ⓗ Ⓢ Ⓤ

Q23 Every Which Way* A53

There are two different ways of completing a 5 × 5 grid so that all five columns, rows and both diagonals contain the numbers 1, 2, 3, 4 and 5; the top row contains the numbers in ascending order; and no diagonal line of two or more squares contains the same number more than once. What are they? (The number 1 has been placed in the first grid as a start.)

Q24 Logic Box* H6, A64
Using the following clues, place the letters A to I inclusive into the grid. C is below G and above E. D is above A and to the right of F which is above I and to the left of G. A is above H and to the right of I. H is to the right of B and to the left of E. ('Above/below' refers to two letters in the same column. 'Left of/right of' refers to two letters in the same row.)

Q25 Grid Fill** H1, A94
Fit the 36 words into the grid below. The letters A and I have been entered into the grid for you as a start.

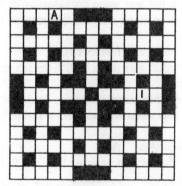

ALLIN ASSAI ATRIP AUDIO BARGE CAIRD

CHANT CHILD DECAL DIVOT DRAIL ENTRY

ESSAY EXERT FEAST INLET IONIC LOCAL

MULTI NEEDY NIECE OCTAL ODEON OMBRE

OMEGA OPTIC OUNCE PILAU RADIO REFER

RELIC TAINT TEMPO TOTAL TWIRL VRAIC

Q26 The Mad Hatter★ H4, A12

Last week the Mad Hatter wore a different style of hat on each day, and each hat was a different colour. Given the following 14 statements, on which day did the Mad Hatter wear the top hat and what colour was the fez?

1. The blue hat was worn on Monday.
2. The cap is yellow.
3. The fez was not worn on Monday or Tuesday.
4. The stetson was worn before the bowler hat and the top hat.
5. The fez is not black.
6. The orange hat was worn before the black hat and after the trilby.
7. The sombrero is not red or blue.
8. The trilby was worn the day after the bowler hat.
9. The black hat was worn on Saturday or Sunday.
10. The trilby is green and the first day of the week is Monday.
11. The top hat is not black or red.
12. The white hat was worn before the fez and after the yellow hat.
13. The bowler hat was not worn on Friday or Saturday.
14. The cap was worn after the trilby and before the fez.

Q27 Odd Ones Out★ A82

Which three cubes cannot be made from the flattened cube shown below?

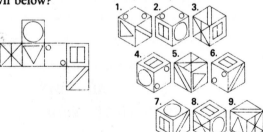

20

Q28 Before or Not Before** H8, A43

My wife Tracey is very keen on English Literature, and has read most of the works of Shakespeare, the last one being *Richard III*. I asked Tracey for a list of the works of Shakespeare that she had read so that I could use the list in a puzzle, but she gave me the list in the following form. Each play she had read was listed on the left-hand side. On the right-hand side was one or more of the plays that she had read after the play shown on the left-hand side. It is possible to construct a list of the plays in the order that my wife read them; what is the correct order?

Play	*Plays read after play shown to the left*
The Taming of the Shrew	*A Midsummer Night's Dream, The Comedy of Errors, The Merchant of Venice, Twelfth Night, Antony and Cleopatra.*
Romeo and Juliet	*As You Like It, Julius Caesar, Troilus and Cressida, The Tempest, Much Ado About Nothing, The Winter's Tale.*
Much Ado About Nothing	*Twelfth Night, The Taming of the Shrew, The Tempest, The Comedy of Errors, King John.*
The Comedy of Errors	*Coriolanus, King John, Twelfth Night, Macbeth, Cymbeline, A Midsummer Night's Dream.*
Julius Caesar	*The Taming of the Shrew, A Midsummer Night's Dream, Merry Wives of Windsor, Timon of Athens, Hamlet, The Comedy of Errors, The*

	Merchant of Venice, Love's Labour's Lost.
Measure for Measure	Love's Labour's Lost, Hamlet, All's Well That Ends Well, Timon of Athens, The Taming of the Shrew, Twelfth Night.
The Merchant of Venice	Hamlet, The Tempest.
Love's Labour's Lost	Troilus and Cressida.
Hamlet	Antony and Cleopatra.
Cymbeline	A Midsummer Night's Dream.
The Winter's Tale	All's Well That Ends Well, Antony and Cleopatra, King John, Measure for Measure, Troilus and Cressida, Much Ado About Nothing.
Two Gentlemen of Verona	As You Like It, Romeo and Juliet, The Winter's Tale.
Merry Wives of Windsor	The Winter's Tale, Much Ado About Nothing, Timon of Athens.
The Tempest	The Comedy of Errors, Twelfth Night.
Timon of Athens	Love's Labour's Lost.
Titus Andronicus	Two Gentlemen of Verona, Julius Caesar, Twelfth Night, The Winter's Tale, Romeo and Juliet.
Troilus and Cressida	Antony and Cleopatra, Much Ado About Nothing.

continued overleaf

Twelfth Night	*A Midsummer Night's Dream, Coriolanus, Cymbeline, Macbeth.*
All's Well That Ends Well	*Love's Labour's Lost, Timon of Athens.*
Antony and Cleopatra	*The Tempest.*
As You Like It	*Julius Caesar, The Winter's Tale, Much Ado About Nothing.*
Coriolanus	*Macbeth.*
King John	*Twelfth Night.*
Macbeth	*Cymbeline, A Midsummer Night's Dream.*

Q29 Auntie Christmas* H4, A26

1. Auntie Carol will not get the flowers unless Auntie Sheila gets the chocolates.
2. Auntie Sheila will not get the chocolates unless Auntie Joan gets the slippers.
3. Auntie Mary will not get the flowers unless Auntie Joan gets the chocolates.
4. Auntie Joan will not get the slippers unless Auntie Carol gets the chocolates.
5. Auntie Joan will not get the voucher unless Auntie Sheila gets the slippers.
6. Auntie Sheila will not get the slippers unless Auntie Mary gets the flowers.
7. Auntie Mary will not get the voucher unless Auntie Carol gets the slippers.
8. Auntie Carol will not get the voucher unless Auntie Sheila gets the flowers.
9. Auntie Sheila will not get the flowers unless Auntie Joan gets the slippers.

10. Auntie Sheila will not get the voucher unless Auntie Carol gets the slippers.

11. Auntie Carol will not get the slippers unless Auntie Joan gets the flowers.

Which Auntie will get the slippers for Christmas?

Q30 Blocked** H7, A2

Each of the 25 blocks of four letters shown below can be rotated about its centre, either 90° clockwise or 90° anti-clockwise. When all of the 25 blocks are in their correct positions, all ten rows and columns contain the letters A to J only once.

Fifteen of the blocks shown below are not in their correct positions. Seven blocks have been rotated clockwise and eight blocks have been rotated anticlockwise. Given that three blocks have been rotated in each of the five rows and columns of blocks, which 15 of the 25 have been rotated and in which direction?

	A	B	C	D	E
1	I F / G E	J H / A B	E G / F H	C A / I C	D B / J D
2	B D / D H	B H / J E	G J / A C	F I / G F	A I / E C
3	G J / J A	F I / C E	D H / C B	B D / A H	I E / F G
4	C A / H C	I G / F D	E B / I J	B D / G E	J H / A F
5	F I / E B	C A / D G	A F / I D	E J / J H	H B / G C

Q31 Square Cut* A32

Divide the square into four parts of equal size and shape, each of which must include the nine letters, S, E, C, T, I, O, N, A and L.

C	L	I	S	T	C
A	O	E	N	I	A
L	N	S	A	C	S
T	I	C	L	N	O
E	O	A	O	S	E
N	T	I	E	L	T

Q32 Done What?* A130

Arthur said Dave did it, Dave said Bill did it, Bill said Charlie did it, Charlie said that he didn't do it and Eddie confessed that he did it. If Arthur didn't do it, one of the five of them did do it and only one of them is telling the truth; who did do it?

Q33 Letter Boxes* H5, A147

When the diagram below is complete, each column and row should contain the letters A, B, C, D, E, F, G, H, I and J. See if you can complete the diagram by fitting the nine blocks of nine letters into the nine highlighted squares and filling in the remaining spaces.

B	J	H
J	D	G
D	I	J

H	F	D
I	B	E
B	A	J

G	I	C
E	C	B
C	G	A

D	E	F
J	H	I
A	D	H

F	A	D
A	I	F
H	F	E

H	B	A
A	E	J
G	F	D

H	J	A
G	B	E
J	G	F

E	D	C
C	B	I
J	C	A

B	C	I
C	A	F
E	I	C

Q34 Colour Cube* A95

A large cube can be made with the 27 smaller cubes shown below, so that each face of the large cube is entirely red, orange, green, yellow, blue or violet.

The faces of the smaller cubes that you cannot see are indigo. Which cubes could be on the top layer, which in the centre layer and which on the bottom layer? Put the numbers of the cubes (left to right, top to bottom) in three 9-box grids. To start you off, nos 1 and 23 are in the top layer.

R = Red
O = Orange
G = Green
B = Blue
Y = Yellow
V = Violet
I = Indigo

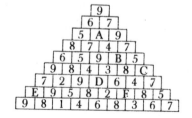

Q35 Number Pyramid* A74

Fill in the missing numbers which have been replaced by the letters A to F.

```
            9
          6   7
        5   A   9
      8   7   4   7
    6   5   9   B   5
  9   8   4   3   8   C
7   2   9   D   6   4   7
E   9   5   8   2   F   8   5
9   8   1   4   6   8   3   6   7
```

26

Q36 Flipover** H3, A109

Diagram One is that of the numbers 1, 2, 3 and 4, each of which is surrounded by eight circles, all of which contain a different letter. The eight circles around each of the four numbers can be 'flipped over' the number itself either vertically or horizontally. For example, in Diagram One, if the letters around the number 1 were flipped vertically, A and F would swap places, B and G would swap places, C and H would swap places and D and E would remain in the same position.

Diagram Two is that of Diagram One after each of the four numbers have been flipped over a total of six times. Each number has been flipped over at least once but no more than twice. In what order, and in which direction, have the letters around each number been flipped over to arrive at the positions shown in Diagram Two?

Diagram One ⒜ⒹⒻⒾⓀⓃⓅⓈⓊ
⒝①⒢②Ⓛ③Ⓞ④ⓋⓋ
ⒸⒺⒽⒿⓂⓄⓇⓉⓌ

Diagram Two ⒸⒺⒻⒾⓂⓃⓌⓈⓇ
⒝①⒢②Ⓛ③Ⓥ④Ⓠ
ⒶⒹⒽⒿⓀⓄⓊⓉⓅ

Q37 Double Wordsquare* A13

Fit the 20 blocks into the two grids to form two different wordsquares which read the same down and across.

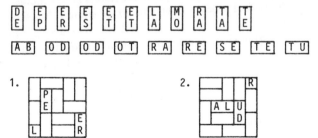

Q38 Connection** A120

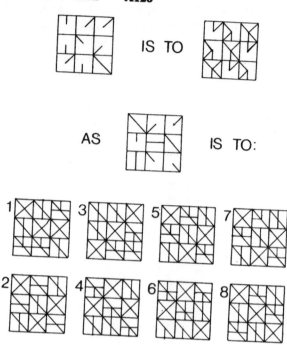

Q39 Logic Box* H6, A22

Using the following clues, place the letters A to I inclusive into the grid. A is below E which is to the left of I. B is above F and D. H is below E and to the left of C. D is above F and to the right of G. ('Above/below' refers to two letters in the same column. 'Left of/right of' refers to two letters in the same row.)

Q40 Monarch E*   H8, A84

Given below is a list of monarchs whose names all begin with the letter E. The list gives the names of some or all of the other monarchs who were monarchs after the monarch whose name is given first in Column One. All you have to do is construct a list of the monarchs in the order in which they became monarchs. As there were quite a few Edwards, if you were given the information as Edward I, Edward II, Edward III etc., it would be too easy; so the Edwards have had their numbers replaced by the number of years they were king. The Elizabeths have been left unchanged.

Column One Name of monarch	Column Two Monarchs who were monarchs after the monarch in column One
Edward the Confessor	Edward (1 year), Edward (35 years), Elizabeth I, Edward (10 years).
Ethelbald	Ethelbert, Ethelred, Ethelred the Unready, Edward (22 years), Edmund Ironside, Edmund.
Edmund Ironside	Elizabeth I, Edward the Confessor, Edward (22 years), Edward (1 year), Edward (6 years).
Edward the Elder	Edmund, Edmund Ironside, Edgar.
Edward (22 years)	Edward (1 year), Elizabeth I.
Edgar	Edward the Martyr.
Egbert	Ethelwulf, Ethelred, Elizabeth I, Edmund, Ethelbald.
Ethelred the Unready	Edward (10 years), Edmund Ironside.
Elizabeth I	Edward (9 years), Elizabeth II, Edward who abdicated.

29

Edmund	Edwig, Edward (10 years), Edward (6 years), Edred, Ethelred the Unready, Edmund Ironside.
Ethelwulf	Ethelbert, Ethelbald, Edmund.
Edwig	Edward the Martyr, Edgar.
Edward (10 years)	Edward (22 years).
Ethelbert	Ethelred, Edmund, Edmund Ironside.
Edward (1 year)	Edward (9 years), Edward (6 years), Elizabeth I, Edward who abdicated, Elizabeth II.
Edward (9 years)	Edward who abdicated.
Ethelred	Edward the Confessor, Edward the Elder, Edgar, Edward (1 year), Edward (35 years), Edward the Martyr, Edward (20 years).
Edward (6 years)	Elizabeth I.
Edward who abdicated	Elizabeth II.
Edred	Edward the Martyr, Edward (20 years), Edwig, Edgar, Edward the Confessor, Elizabeth I.
Edward (35 years)	Edward (20 years), Edward (22 years).
Edward the Martyr	Ethelred the Unready.
Edward (20 years)	Edward (10 years).

Q41 Odd One Out** A44

The diagrams below are that of a flattened cube and three views of the cube before it was flattened. Which of the three views is incorrect? (The cube can be restored to its original form by folding along the dotted lines. None of the three views show the edges of the diagram of the flattened cube.)

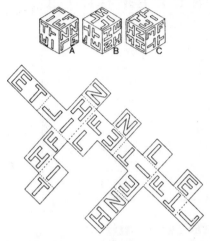

Q42 Laser Maze** H2, A54

The diagram below represents an aerial view of a room which has been divided into 100 squares, as shown by the dotted lines. In each of the squares there should be a dot marked on the floor in the centre of the square, or a double-sided mirror. When all of the dots and mirrors are in their correct places, a laser beam can enter the room at square A1 in the direction indicated by an arrow, and leave the room from square J10. At the same time, the laser beam shines over each and every dot marked on the floor. When the beam reaches a mirror it 'bounces off' at an angle of 90°, but it never crosses itself. If the beam hits the outside wall it is absorbed by the wall and can go no further. In the room below only one side of a mirror is ever used.

Fourteen of the dots/mirrors are not in place: four dots (X), seven mirrors from lower left to upper right (Y), and three mirrors from upper left to lower right (Z). See if you can determine which of the squares containing '?' should be replaced by: 1. X squares; 2. Y squares; 3. Z squares.

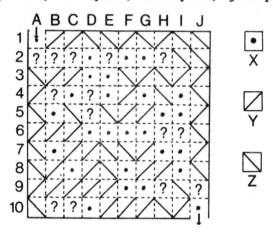

Q43 All The Twos* A131

Alex, Brad, Colin, Doug, Eric and Frank had a race to school from the bus-stop and then another race from school to the bus-stop. In the first race, Brad wasn't last and Eric finished before Colin. Frank wasn't first but finished before Doug. Brad finished before Frank but after Alex and Colin. Alex finished four places ahead of Doug. In the second race Alex finished two places ahead of Doug and before Eric who in turn was two places behind Colin. Alex wasn't first and nor was Brad who finished before Eric. Frank finished one place ahead of Doug.

From the information given:

1. Which two boys finished in a better position in the first race than in the second race?

2. Which two boys finished in the same position in the second race as they did in the first race?

Q44 People's Pets* H4, A96

Consider the following.

1. Five men each have different first names and different surnames, have five different pets and live at five different addresses. All five pets have a different name.
2. Tom's surname is Williams and the fish is not called Spike, Benson or Rodney.
3. Harry has a pet cat and the budgie is called Percy.
4. George's surname is not Hudson or Smith.
5. Mr Thompson owns the dog and the owner of the rabbit lives in Pine Avenue.
6. The cat is not called Benson and one of the five men has a pet called Fred.
7. Mr Anderson does not live in Cedar Road.
8. Mr Hudson lives in Willow Street.
9. Mr Anderson owns a pet called Percy and John lives in Cedar Road.
10. Bill's pet is called Rodney and is not the dog; the owner of the fish lives in Maple Grove.

Who lives in Chestnut Crescent and what is the name of their pet?

Q45 The Animals Went In Which Way?** H8, A65

The animals may have gone into Noah's Ark two by two, but in which order did they go in? Given the following sentence (yes, sentence! – I make no apologies for the punctuation), what was the order in which the animals entered the Ark?

The monkeys went in before the sheep, swans, chickens, peacocks, geese, penguins and spiders, but went in after the horses, badgers, squirrels and tigers, the latter of which went in before the horses, the penguins, the rabbits, the pigs, the donkeys, the snakes and the mice, but the mice went before the leopards, the leopards before the squirrels,

the squirrels before the chickens, the chickens before the
penguins, spiders, sheep, geese and the peacocks, the
peacocks before the geese and the penguins, the penguins
before the spiders and after the geese and the horses, the
horses before the donkeys, the chickens and the leopards,
the leopards after the foxes and the ducks, the ducks before
the goats, swans, doves, foxes and badgers, the badgers
before the chickens, horses, squirrels and swans and after
the lions, foxes, rabbits and beavers, the beavers before the
lions, tigers, foxes, squirrels and ducks, the ducks after the
lions, elephants, rabbits and otters, the otters before the
elephants, tigers, chickens and beavers, the beavers after
the elephants, the elephants before the lions, the lions
before the tigers, the sheep before the peacocks, the swans
before the chickens, the pigs before the snakes, the snakes
before the foxes, the pigs after the rabbits, goats, tigers and
doves, the doves before the chickens, horses, goats, donkeys and snakes, the snakes after the goats, and the donkeys
before the mice and the squirrels.

Q46 Mix Up Square* H9, A3

Complete the square so that all of the columns and rows
contain the letters:

S Q U A R E

Each of the six letters must only appear once in each column
or row.

S	Q	U	A	R	E
E					
Q	E			A	
A			S		
	U				Q
		R		E	S

Q47 Odd Block Out* A141
Which is the odd block out?

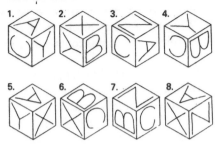

Q48 Grid Fill** H1, A38
Fit the 36 words into the grid below.

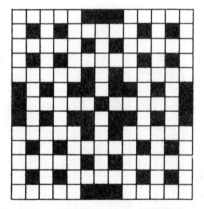

ALLOT AMENT AMORT ARISE ATLAS CAROL

DOLCE ELDER EMEND EVENS EVENT EXILE

HAREM IDLER IMAGE LATER LINER NEWEL

NOISE OKAPI OPINE REVUE RINSE ROOST

SOWER SPENT STALE TATER THEIR THEME

TREAT VENUE VILLA VISIT YEAST YODEL

Q49 Blocked** H7, A149

Each of the 25 blocks of four letters shown below can be rotated about its centre, either 90° clockwise, 90° anticlockwise or 180°. When all of the 25 blocks are in their correct positions, all ten rows and columns contain the letters A to J only once.

Fifteen of the blocks shown below are not in their correct positions. Five blocks have been rotated clockwise, five blocks have been rotated anticlockwise and five blocks have been rotated 180°. Given that each of the five rows and columns of blocks contain three blocks which have been rotated, no two of which have been rotated the same way, which 15 of the 25 have been rotated and in which direction?

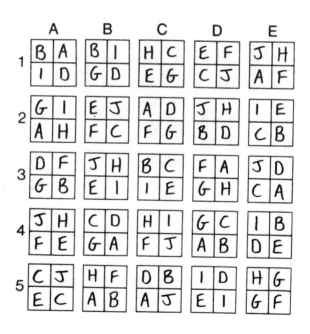

36

Q50 Logicalympics – 100 Metres* H4, A110

The logicalympics take place every year in a very quiet setting so that the competitors can concentrate on their events – not so much the events themselves, but the results. At the logicalympics every event ends in a tie so that no one goes home disappointed. There were five entries in the 100m, so they held five races in order that each competitor could win, and so that each competitor could also take his/her turn in 2nd, 3rd, 4th and 5th place. The final results showed that each competitor had duly taken their turn in finishing in each of the five positions. Given the following information, what were the results of each of the five races?

The five competitors were A, B, C, D and E. C didn't win the fourth race. In the first race A finished before C who in turn finished after B. A finished in a better position in the fourth race than in the second race. E didn't win the second race. E finished two places behind C in the first race. D lost the fourth race. A finished ahead of B in the fourth race, but B finished before A and C in the third race. A had already finished before C in the second race who in turn finished after B again. B was not first in the first race and D was not last. D finished in a better position in the second race than in the first race and finished before B. A wasn't second in the second race and also finished before B.

Q51 Uncle Christmas* H4, A121

1. Uncle Raymond will not get the scarf unless Uncle John gets the hat.
2. Uncle George will not get the gloves unless Uncle Victor gets the scarf.
3. Uncle Victor will not get the tie unless Uncle George gets the scarf.
4. Uncle John will not get the gloves unless Uncle Raymond gets the hat.

5. Uncle John will not get the hat unless Uncle Victor gets the gloves.
6. Uncle George will not get the hat unless Uncle Raymond gets the tie.
7. Uncle George will not get the tie unless Uncle Raymond gets the hat.
8. Uncle Raymond will not get the hat unless Uncle George gets the scarf.
9. Uncle Victor will not get the gloves unless Uncle Raymond gets the hat.
10. Uncle John will not get the tie unless Uncle Raymond gets the gloves.
11. Uncle George will not get the scarf unless Uncle Raymond gets the gloves.

Which Uncle will get the scarf for Christmas?

Q52 Number Fill* A75

Given that the same number does not appear in two adjacent squares, either vertically, horizontally or diagonally, fit the numbers 1 to 9 inclusive four times each into the 6 × 6 grid. Only one number should be entered into each of the 36 squares. Some of the numbers appear next to the row and/or beneath the column into which they should be placed.

grid									
						5	6	9	
						2	2	3	7 8
						5	5	6	
						2	2	3	9 7
						1	4	5	8 8
						3	3	6	7 9 9

4	1	1	2	1	1
4	2	6	2	6	3
7	2	6	3	7	3
8	5	9	5	8	4
8	7	9	5	8	4
9	7	9	5		

38

Q53 Coin Puzzle* A55

Move one coin so that there are two straight lines of six coins which cross each other at the centre point of each line.

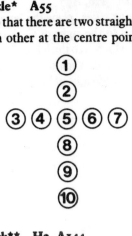

Q54 Clockwork** H3, A144

Diagram One is that of the numbers 1, 2, 3 and 4, each of which is surrounded by eight circles, all of which contain a different letter. The eight circles around each of the four numbers can be rotated either 90° clockwise, 90° anticlockwise or 180°. For example, if 1 were to be rotated 90° clockwise, the letter A would replace the letter F, D would replace G, F would replace H, G would replace E, H would replace C, etc.

Diagram Two is that of Diagram One after seven rotations of the letters around the four numbers – two clockwise, two anticlockwise and three through 180°. The letters around each number have been rotated at least once but no more than twice. In what order, and in which direction, have the letters around each number been rotated in Diagram One to arrive at the position shown in Diagram Two?

Diagram One

Ⓐ Ⓓ Ⓕ Ⓘ Ⓚ Ⓝ Ⓟ Ⓢ Ⓤ
Ⓑ ① Ⓖ ② Ⓛ ③ Ⓠ ④ Ⓥ
Ⓒ Ⓔ Ⓗ Ⓙ Ⓜ Ⓞ Ⓡ Ⓣ Ⓦ

Diagram Two

Ⓕ Ⓔ Ⓐ Ⓑ Ⓦ Ⓥ Ⓡ Ⓠ Ⓟ
① ① Ⓖ ② Ⓝ ③ Ⓣ ④ Ⓢ
Ⓚ Ⓓ Ⓤ Ⓞ Ⓜ Ⓙ Ⓗ Ⓛ Ⓒ

Q55 Logic Box★ H6, A97

Using the following clues, place the letters A to I inclusive into the grid. E is to the right of C. A is to the right of G which is above B which is to the left of F. I is above D which is to the left of G. ('Above/below' refers to two letters in the same column. 'Left of/right of' refers to two letters in the same row.)

Q56 What Next?★ A14

Find the next most appropriate square:

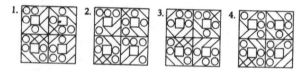

Choose from:

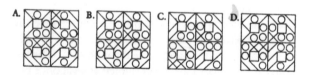

Q57 Grouping★ A45

To which group does the letter J belong?
1. F G
2. B C D E
3. A
4. H I

Neil is younger than Matthew. Barry is older than Robert
and Dave. Dave is older than Joe who is younger than John
and Philip. Arthur is older than Paul who is older than
Matthew. Robert is older than Dave. Martin is older than
Simon. George is also older than Simon but younger than
Martin. Bill is older than Jimmy and Tom but younger than
Harry. Harry is also older than Tom. Tcin is older than
Arthur, Dave and Eddie but younger than Jimmy. Keith is
older than Barry. Neil is younger than Kevin and older than
Frank. Paul is also older than Frank. Simon is older than
Ian. Ian is older than Neil and Colin. Colin is older than
John but younger than Eddie. Kevin is older than Martin
and Michael.

John is younger than Michael. Keith and Dave are younger than John. Philip is older than Keith. Jimmy and Bill
are younger than Leonard. Harry is older than Leonard.
Michael and John are younger than Philip. Philip is older
than Barry. Arthur is older than Neil. Frank and Colin are
younger than Bill. John is older than Robert. Robert is
younger than Philip who is older than Dave. Arthur is also
older than Dave. Kevin and Colin are younger than Jimmy.
Leonard is older than Kevin who is younger than Bill. Ian is
also younger than Bill. Tom is older than Paul, Simon and
Matthew. Fred is also older than Simon and Matthew.

George is younger than Tom and Fred. Kevin is older
than Fred and Colin. Colin is older than Arthur and Frank.
Arthur is older than Philip. Philip is younger than Colin.
Arthur, Frank and Fred are older than John. Eddie is older
than Kevin and George. Colin is older than Michael. Philip
and John are younger than Frank. Harry is older than
Kevin. Barry is younger than John. Ian is younger than
Kevin. Tom is older than Philip. Martin and Arthur are
younger than Fred.

Using the information given above, list all of the people
mentioned in order of age, oldest first.

Q59 Letter Boxes* H5, A27

When the diagram below is complete, each column and row should contain the letters A, B, C, D, E, F, G, H, I and J. See if you can complete the diagram by fitting the nine blocks of nine letters into the nine highlighted squares and filling in the remaining spaces.

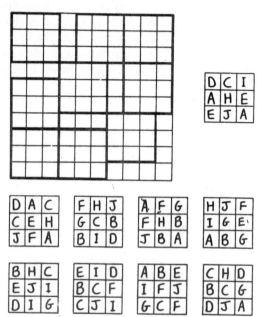

Q60 Done What?* A132

George said Arthur did it, Arthur said Bill did it, Bill said Charlie did it, Charlie said Fred did it, Eddie said Fred did it so Fred confessed and said that he did do it. Harry said Eddie did it, Dave then confessed and said that he did it so John also confessed and said that he did it. Finally, Ian said that he didn't do it. If George didn't do it, one of the ten of them did do it and only one of them is telling the truth; who did do it?

Q61 Odd One Out** A4

The diagrams below are that of a flattened cube and three
views of the cube before it was flattened. Which of the three
views is incorrect? (The cube can be restored to its original
form by folding along the dotted lines.)

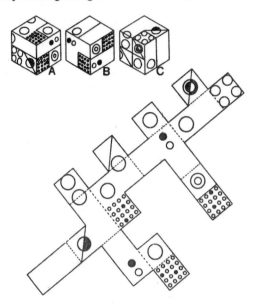

Q62 Wordsquares* A33

Fit the 16 words into the four grids to form four word-
squares which read the same down and across.

AGAR DOTE EDGE ELSE ENOW HOME IDEA LIMP
MEAL MEMO MERE OPEN ORAL PALE TASS TEAM

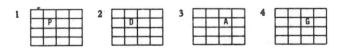

Q63 Connection** A98

IS TO

AS

IS TO:

1 2 3 4 5 6

Q64 Safecracker* A139

The combination of a safe consists of the numbers 1, 2, 3 and 4. There are only the four numbers in the combination but the safe is computerised and changes the combination each time it is closed. Each number appears only once in each combination. The person opening the safe is only allowed four attempts, after which the safe cannot be opened for at least 48 hours. When you tap in the combination on the push-button panel, there is a display next to the panel which indicates the number of numbers you have 'tapped in' in the correct position. The last time that I opened the safe I tapped in the following combinations; on my first attempt I tapped in 3 1 2 4, none of which were in the correct place. I then tapped in 2 3 4 1; again none of the numbers were in the correct place. On my third attempt I only tapped in the number 1 in first place; the safe indicated that it was not in the correct place, after which I then knew the combination. What was the correct combination?

44

Q65   Jack Of All Trades***   H8, A66

My friend Jack asked me if I would help him prepare a new C.V. for a job he had seen advertised in a newspaper. I asked him what jobs he had had since leaving school. He said his first job was as a journalist and his present job was as a scene-shifter, but, although he could remember the various jobs he had had, he couldn't remember the order in which he had had them. I told him to tell me what he could remember and then I would try to prepare a list of the jobs he had had in the correct order.

This is what he said: 'After being a journalist I was a signwriter, an illustrator, a compositor and a pawnbroker, but I was a pawnbroker before I was a ringmaster, a piano-tuner and an interpreter. Before I was an interpreter I was a chargehand, and after I was an interpreter I was a compositor. I can remember being a compositor before I was a gamekeeper, a taxi-driver, an electrician and a roadsweeper. I was a gamekeeper and an electrician after I was a roadsweeper which in turn was after I was a taxi-driver and a woodcarver. I liked my job as a woodcarver which I got after being a blacksmith, a chargehand, a lumberjack and an illustrator. I was an illustrator after I had a job as a cartoonist and an undertaker, and I was an undertaker before I was a pawnbroker and a chargehand but after I was a signwriter and a cartoonist.

'I can also remember being a fishmonger, a lumberjack, a chargehand and a pawnbroker after I was a cartoonist which in turn was after I was a journalist and a signwriter. I was a signwriter before I was a pawnbroker, a pawnbroker before I was an upholsterer, an upholsterer before I was a programmer, a programmer before I was a fishmonger, a fishmonger before I was a piano-tuner and a chargehand, a chargehand before I was a blacksmith, and a blacksmith before I was a gamekeeper, an escapologist, a compositor and a piano-tuner. I was a piano-tuner before I was a lumberjack but that was after I had been a chargehand and an escapologist. I was also a greengrocer after being an upholsterer and an illustrator. Then again, I can also remember being a greengrocer after I was an escapologist but before I was a piano-tuner.

'At one time I was a postmaster but that was before I was a pawnbroker, a chargehand and a newscaster which in turn was after I was an illustrator. I had quite a few jobs after I was an illustrator, including being a blacksmith, a gamekeeper, a newscaster, an escapologist and a programmer. One thing that I do know is that I haven't done the same type of job twice. As I said before, I liked my job as a woodcarver but that was before I was a taxi-driver, an interpreter, a compositor, a gamekeeper and an electrician. I was actually an electrician before I was a gamekeeper.

'One job that I wasn't too keen on was that time I was an upholsterer, but that was before I was a ringmaster, a newscaster, a blacksmith and a compositor. I was a compositor after I was a chargehand and a lumberjack. One quite boring job was that of a programmer which was after I was a newscaster and a ringmaster, and I was a ringmaster before I was a newscaster. The only other things I can remember is that I was a chargehand after I was a fishmonger and a pawnbroker, and that I was a pawnbroker before I was a fishmonger.'

Given what Jack said, see if you can make a list of the jobs he has had since being a journalist and the order in which he has had them.

Each of the 25 blocks of four letters shown below can be rotated about its centre, either 90° clockwise, 90° anticlockwise or 180°. When all of the 25 blocks are in their correct positions, all ten rows and columns contain the letters A to J only once.

Thirteen of the blocks shown below are not in their correct positions. Given that each of the five rows and columns of blocks contains at least one and no more than four blocks which have been rotated, which 13 of the 25 have been rotated and in which direction(s)?

	A	B	C	D	E
1	H J / B H	F D / C A	F I / E B	D G / A I	J C / E G
2	A G / F E	J I / G D	C H / A C	F E / I B	J H / B D
3	G D / E B	F H / I B	J G / A J	C D / E C	H F / A I
4	C I / I F	A J / C E	H D / D B	H B / J G	F E / G A
5	A D / C J	G B / E H	F E / I G	F J / H A	C I / B D

Q67 Piano Lessons* AIII

Complete the timetable shown below for next week's piano lessons, using the following information.

1. Brian has a grade one lesson on Monday and Tuesday.
2. Susan does not have a lesson on Wednesday or Thursday.
3. Tommy has a lesson on Thursday.
4. There are no grade one, three or five lessons on Friday.
5. Both Susan and Lucy have two lessons next week.
6. Julie has a grade three lesson the day after Jill has a grade five lesson which is not on Monday.
7. There are no grade one or grade three lessons on Wednesday.

8. Susan has a grade two lesson in the afternoon of the same day in which Lucy has a grade four lesson.

9. There is a grade three lesson on Thursday afternoon and a grade one lesson on Thursday morning.

10. There are no grade five lessons on an afternoon.

11. John has a grade three lesson in the afternoon of the day before Susan has her grade two lesson.

12. No-one has two lessons on the same day.

| | MORNING | | AFTERNOON | |
	NAME	GRADE	NAME	GRADE
MONDAY				
TUESDAY				
WEDNESDAY				
THURSDAY				
FRIDAY				

Q68 Mix Up Squared* H9, A46

Complete the square so that all of the columns and rows contain the letters:

S Q U A R E D

Each of the seven letters must only appear once in each column or row.

S	Q	U	A	R	E	D
	A				G	
D		Q	R			
			E			
	E	R	Q			
E						S
		A			S	R

Q69 Logic Box* H6, A122

Using the following clues, place the letters A to I inclusive into the grid. A is below B which is to the right of H and above C which is to the left of G which is below E and above F which is to the right of I. ('Above/below' refers to two letters in the same column. 'Left of/right of' refers to two letters in the same row.)

Q70 Clockwork** H3, A23

Diagram One is that of the numbers 1, 2, 3 and 4, each of which is surrounded by eight circles, all of which contain a different letter. The eight circles around each of the four numbers can be rotated either 90° clockwise, 90° anticlock-. wise or 180°. For example, if 1 were to be rotated 90° clockwise, the letter A would replace the letter F, D would replace G, F would replace H, G would replace E, H would replace C, etc.

Diagram Two is that of Diagram One after seven rotations of the letters around the four numbers—two clockwise, two anticlockwise and three through 180°. The letters around each number have been rotated at least once but no more than twice. In what order, and in what direction, have the letters around each number been rotated in Diagram One to arrive at the positions shown in Diagram Two?

Diagram One

Ⓐ Ⓓ Ⓕ Ⓘ Ⓚ Ⓝ Ⓟ Ⓢ Ⓤ
Ⓑ ① Ⓖ ② Ⓛ ③ Ⓠ ④ Ⓥ
Ⓒ Ⓔ Ⓗ Ⓙ Ⓜ Ⓞ Ⓡ Ⓣ Ⓦ

Diagram Two

Ⓗ Ⓔ Ⓟ Ⓢ Ⓚ Ⓘ Ⓒ Ⓞ Ⓤ
Ⓖ ① Ⓙ ② Ⓝ ③ Ⓠ ④ Ⓥ
Ⓕ Ⓓ Ⓜ Ⓛ Ⓐ Ⓑ Ⓡ Ⓣ Ⓦ

49

Q71 Number Fill* A15

Given that the same number does not appear in two adjacent squares, either vertically, horizontally or diagonally, fit the numbers 1 to 12 inclusive four times each into the grid below. Only one number should be entered into each square. Some of the numbers appear next to the row and/or beneath the column into which they should be placed.

1	1	3	3	8	10	12
2	7	7	7	7	10	12
1	3	3	4	5	9	10
2	5	6	8	11	11	
2	4	5	9	9	11	12
1	2	5	6	8	10	12
4	4	6	6	8	9	11

2	2	5	3	1	3
2	5	8	3	1	3
5	8	9		1	4
6	8	11		5	6
10	9	12		9	6
10		12		9	11
10				10	

Q72 Consider* A58

Consider the following diagram:

Which of the following six diagrams is the odd one out?

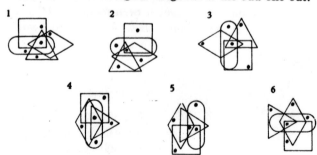

50

Q73 Square Cut* A86

Divide the square into four parts of equal size and shape, each of which must include one A, one B and one C.

		A	A	A	
		B	B	C	C
	A		B		
				B	
C	C				

Q74 Whodunnit?** H4, A99

Lord Logic was found lying dead on the kitchen floor. Next to the body was a hammer, a vase and a truncheon. There were four people in the kitchen, apart from the dead body, when the police arrived; Lady Logic, Lord Logic's mistress, the butler and the maid. There were five detectives working on the case, each of whom took a statement from all four suspects. Given that only 10 of the 20 statements given were true, who killed Lord Logic, and with what?

Detective	Suspect	Statement given by suspect
1	Butler	The maid killed Lord Logic with the hammer.
1	Maid	The butler killed Lord Logic with the vase.
1	Lady Logic	Lord Logic's mistress did not kill him with the hammer.
1	Mistress	I killed Lord Logic with the vase.
2	Butler	Lady Logic hit Lord Logic over the head with the hammer and killed him.
2	Maid	The butler killed Lord Logic using the truncheon.

2	Lady Logic	The butler killed Lord Logic using the vase.
2	Mistress	Lady Logic did not kill Lord Logic with the vase.
3	Butler	Lord Logic's mistress did not kill him with the vase.
3	Maid	Lady Logic used the vase to kill Lord Logic.
3	Lady Logic	My husband's mistress did not kill him with a truncheon.
3	Mistress	Lady Logic killed her husband by hitting him on the back of the head with the hammer.
4	Butler	Lord Logic was killed by his mistress. She hit him over the head with the truncheon.
4	Maid	Lady Logic did not kill her husband with the truncheon.
4	Lady Logic	The maid killed my husband with the vase.
4	Mistress	The butler did it, he killed Lord Logic with the truncheon.
5	Butler	The maid did not kill Lord Logic with the truncheon.
5	Maid	Lady Logic killed her husband with the hammer.
5	Lady Logic	I killed my husband with the hammer.
5	Mistress	The maid hit Lord Logic with the vase and killed him.

Q75 Grid Fill** H1, A5
Fit the 36 words into the grid below.

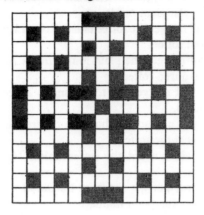

AGATE ALPHA   AROSE ATOLL CAMEL CHAIR

COMET COUCH   CRAZE DURRA EATEN ECLAT

ERODE ERROR   EXTRA HIPPO LADEN LUCRE

MANIC MANOR   NEVER OARED REEST REEVE

RENTE RIVET   SENSE SHRED SLEEP STEIN

THREE TOWEL   TROPE UREDO USAGE WORST

Q76 Somewhere* A140
You have been left in the middle of an island on which there
are two villages. In village A, all of the residents, no matter
where they are, always tell the truth. In village B, all of the
residents, no matter where they are, always tell lies. After
walking a few miles from the middle of the island you find
yourself in a village square where there is a resident of one of
the villages sitting on some stone steps. What one question
would you ask the resident so that you would know which of
the two villages you were in?

Q77 Sweet Tooth** H4, A112

1. Tracey will not get the chocolate-covered mints unless Neil has the plain mints.
2. Alan will not get the toffee unless Robert has the mint-flavoured toffee.
3. Neil will not get the plain mints unless Alan has the mint-flavoured toffee.
4. Robert will not get the toffee unless Tracey gets the plain mints.
5. Robert will not get the chocolate-covered mints unless Tracey gets the toffee.
6. Tracey will not get the toffee unless Neil gets the chocolate.
7. Robert will not get the mint-flavoured toffee unless James gets the plain mints.
8. Alan will not get the plain mints unless Tracey gets the toffee.
9. Tracey will not get the plain mints unless Alan gets the chocolate-covered mints.
10. Alan will not get the mint-flavoured toffee unless Tracey gets the chocolate-covered mints.
11. James will not get the plain mints unless Tracey gets the toffee.
12. Neil will not get the chocolate unless Alan gets the chocolate-covered mints.
13. Robert will not get the plain mints unless James gets the toffee.
14. James will not get the toffee unless Tracey gets the plain mints.
15. Neil will not get the chocolate unless Tracey gets the toffee.
16. Tracey will not get the plain mints unless Robert gets the toffee.
17. Alan will not get the chocolate-covered mints unless James gets the plain mints.

Who will get what?

Q78 Gruffs*** H8, A39

The reporter for the local *Gazette* was at the national dog show yesterday. Unfortunately he also had to report on quite a few other events on the same day. He made some notes when he was at the dog show which are shown below, but the editor of the *Gazette* has asked for a list of the 26 finalists and the positions in which they finished overall. Using the reporter's notes below, see if you can construct the list for the editor, as the reporter didn't have time to make a note of the overall positions.

The Afghan Hound finished before the Alsatian, the Poodle and the Beagle. The Beagle finished before the Bull Mastiff and the Labrador. The Labrador finished before the Poodle and the Pug. The Pug finished before the Alsatian, the Dobermann Pinscher, the St Bernard, the Sheepdog and the Griffon. The Griffon finished before the Sheepdog. The Sheepdog finished after the Poodle. The Poodle finished before the St Bernard, the Collie, the Pug, the Griffon, the Alsatian and the Dobermann Pinscher. The Dobermann Pinscher finished after the Alsatian. The Alsatian finished after the Chow. The Chow finished before the Afghan Hound, the Bulldog, the Chihuahua, the Poodle, the Beagle and the Dachshund. The Dachshund finished before the Spaniel. The Spaniel finished before the Foxhound.

The Foxhound finished before the Labrador. The Labrador finished after the Whippet. The Whippet finished before the Great Dane. The Great Dane finished after the Bull Terrier and before the Chow. The Chow finished before the Bull Mastiff. The Bull Mastiff finished before the Foxhound. The Foxhound finished after the Yorkshire Terrier. The Yorkshire Terrier finished before the Greyhound. The Greyhound finished before the Dachshund. The Dachshund finished after the King Charles Spaniel. The King Charles Spaniel finished before the Bull Mastiff, the Greyhound, the Pug, the Chihuahua and the

Afghan Hound. The Afghan Hound finished after the Dalmatian. The Dalmatian finished before the Pug, the Labrador, the Poodle and the Collie.

The Collie finished before the Pug. The Pug finished after the Retriever. The Retriever finished before the Bull Terrier, the Chow, the Yorkshire Terrier and the Whippet. The Whippet finished before the Chow, the Spaniel, the Dalmatian and the Yorkshire Terrier. The Yorkshire Terrier finished after the Bulldog. The Bulldog finished before the Chihuahua and the Dalmatian. The Dalmatian finished after the Great Dane. The Great Dane finished before the Yorkshire Terrier. The Yorkshire Terrier finished before the Collie, the King Charles Spaniel, the Spaniel and the Dalmatian. The Dalmatian finished after the Spaniel. The Griffon finished before the Alsatian. The Alsatian finished after the Sheepdog. The Griffon finished after the St Bernard. The Greyhound finished before the Chihuahua. The Chihuahua finished before the Dachshund. The Bull Terrier finished before the Whippet and the Yorkshire Terrier. The Afghan Hound finished before the Pug and the Foxhound.

Q79 Odd Block Out* A100
Which is the odd block out?

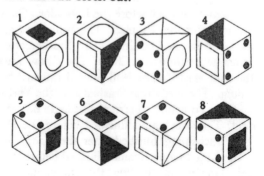

Q80 Odd One Out** A133

The diagrams below are that of a flattened cube and three
views of the cube before it was flattened. Which of the three
views is incorrect? (The cube can be restored to its original
form by folding along the dotted lines.)

Q81 ' Logic Box* H6, A67

Using the following clues, place the letters A to I inclusive
into the grid. C is below D which is to the left of H and to the
right of B which is to the left of H which is above E and A. F
is to the right of G which is below I which is to the left of E.
('Above/below' refers to two letters in the same column.
'Left of/right of' refers to two letters in the same row.)

Q82 Boxed* H4, A123

There are four boxes on a shelf, all in a straight horizontal line. Each box contains a pair of gloves and a scarf. No box contains a pair of gloves and scarf the same colour as the box or each other. All four boxes, pairs of gloves and scarves are either red, green, blue or yellow. No two boxes are the same colour, no two scarves are the same colour and no two pairs of gloves are the same colour.

The red scarf is in the box next to the box containing the pair of green gloves. The yellow gloves are in the box next to the green box which is next to the box containing the green scarf. The box on the far left is red. The blue gloves are in the box next to the box containing the blue scarf. The yellow box isn't next to the blue box which is next to the box containing the red gloves. The green scarf is in the blue box or the yellow box. The yellow scarf is not in the red box which is not, and is not next to, the box containing the yellow gloves.

From the information given, see if you can determine the position of each box on the shelf, what the colour of each box is, and the colour of the gloves and scarf each box contains.

Q83 Wordsquares* A87

Fit the 16 words into the four grids to form four word-squares which read the same down and across.

AGED AMEN AREA DAME DEMO EARN EDEN ENOW

ERNE MADE MANE MERE MORE NEAR NEED OMEN

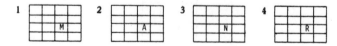

58

Q84 Letter Boxes* H5, A146

When the diagram below is complete, each column and row and one of the diagonals should contain the letters A, B, C, D, E, F, G, H, I and J. See if you can complete the diagram by fitting the eight blocks of nine letters into the eight highlighted squares and filling in the remaining spaces.

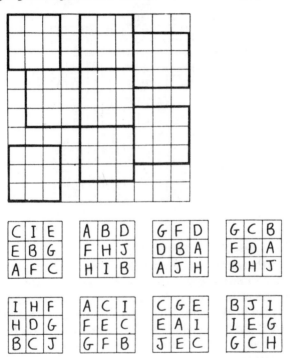

Q85 Blocked** H7, A56

Each of the 25 blocks of four letters shown below can be rotated about its centre, either 90° clockwise or 90° anti-clockwise. When all of the 25 blocks are in their correct positions, all ten rows and columns contain the letters A to J only once.

Twenty of the blocks shown below are not in their correct positions. Given that each of the five rows and columns of blocks contain one block which has not been rotated, ten blocks have been rotated clockwise and ten blocks have been rotated anticlockwise, which 20 of the 25 have been rotated and in which direction?

	A	B	C	D	E
1	A F / G H	C B / E C	H D / A G	D J / J F	I B / E I
2	D G / F I	H A / I J	G C / H J	E B / B E	C F / D A
3	C H / I J	D J / G E	B E / C F	A G / I H	B F / A D
4	D B / A C	I F / F A	I J / E B	H C / D G	E H / G J
5	E B / J E	D G / H B	D F / I A	I C / F A	C C / J H

Q86   Logic Box*   H6, A28

Using the information given below, place the letters A to P inclusive into the grid of 16 squares. L is above J which is to the right of H. O is above C and H and below I which is to the left of B. M is to the left of D and below G. N is below E, above D and to the right of A which is above G, below P and to the right of O and F. ('Above/below' refers to two letters in the same column. 'Left of/right of' refers to two letters in the same row.)

Q87 Connection* A77

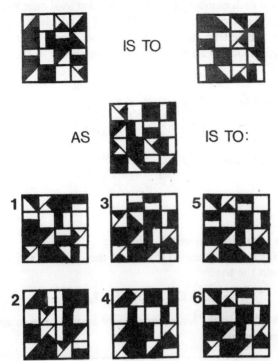

Q88 Clockwork** H3, A16

Diagram One is that of the numbers 1, 2, 3 and 4, each of which is surrounded by eight circles, all of which contain a different letter. The eight circles around each of the four numbers can be rotated either 90° clockwise, 90° anticlockwise or 180°. For example, if 1 were to be rotated 90° clockwise, the letter A would replace the letter F, D would replace G, F would replace H, G would replace E, H would replace C, etc.

Diagram Two is that of Diagram One after seven rotations of the letters around the four numbers – three clockwise, three anticlockwise and one through 180°. The letters around each number have been rotated at least once but no more than twice. In what order, and in which direction, have the letters around each number been rotated in Diagram One to arrive at the positions shown in Diagram Two?

Diagram One

Ⓐ	Ⓓ	Ⓕ	Ⓘ	Ⓚ	Ⓝ	Ⓟ	Ⓢ	Ⓤ
Ⓑ	①	Ⓖ	②	Ⓛ	③	Ⓞ	④	Ⓥ
Ⓒ	Ⓔ	Ⓗ	Ⓙ	Ⓜ	Ⓞ	Ⓡ	Ⓣ	Ⓦ

Diagram Two

Ⓒ	Ⓑ	Ⓗ	Ⓖ	Ⓜ	Ⓛ	Ⓦ	Ⓣ	Ⓡ
Ⓔ	①	Ⓝ	②	Ⓞ	③	Ⓥ	④	Ⓠ
Ⓚ	Ⓙ	Ⓥ	Ⓘ	Ⓟ	Ⓢ	Ⓕ	Ⓖ	Ⓐ

Q89 Mix Up Squarely* H9, A47

Complete the square so that all of the columns and rows contain the letters:

S   Q   U   A   R   E   L   Y

Each of the eight letters must only appear once in each column or row.

S	Q	U	A	R	E	L	Y
R	L		E				S
					Y		E
	R	E			S	U	
Y			L	S		Q	U
	A		Q				
				Q	U	S	
A			S			Y	L

62

Q90 Laser Maze★★ H2, A6

The diagram below represents an aerial view of a room which has been divided into 100 squares, as shown by the dotted lines. In each of the squares there should be a dot marked on the floor of the centre of the square, or a double-sided mirror. When all of the dots and mirrors are in their correct places, a laser beam can enter the room at square A1 in the direction indicated by an arrow, and leave the room from square J10. At the same time, the laser beam shines over each and every dot marked on the floor. When the beam reaches a mirror it 'bounces off' at an angle of 90°, but it never crosses itself. If the beam hits the outside wall it is absorbed by the wall and can go no further.

Sixteen of the dots/mirrors are not in place: three dots (X), five mirrors from lower left to upper right (Y), and eight mirrors from upper left to lower right (Z). See if you can determine which of the squares containing '?' should be replaced by:

1. X squares.   2. Y squares.   3. Z squares.

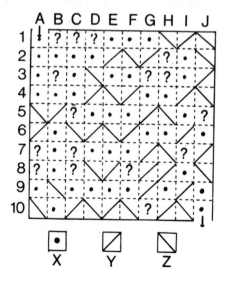

63

Q91 Father Unlike Son* H4, A34

There is one grandfather, one father (not counting the grandfather) and one son (not counting the father) in each of the Smith, Jones and Brown families. Each of the nine is either a plumber, a joiner or a bricklayer. Grandfather Smith is a joiner and no-one with the surname Jones has a son or grandson who is a bricklayer, but someone with the surname Brown has a father who is a bricklayer. Also, no-one has the same occupation as his father, grandfather, son or grandson. Given that no two grandfathers, fathers or sons have the same occupation, what is the occupation of the Jones son who isn't a father?

Q92 Odd One Out** A17

The diagrams below are that of a flattened cube and three views of the cube before it was flattened. Which of the three views is incorrect? (The cube can be restored to its original form by folding along the dotted lines.)

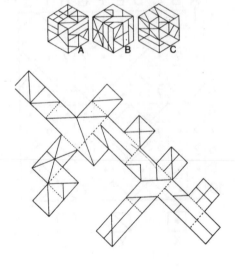

Q93 What Colour Next?*** H8, A57

My next-door neighbour paints his garden fence a different colour every two weeks. Last year he painted his fence 26 different colours. Given the following information, in what order, colourwise, did my neighbour paint his fence last year?

He painted the fence Coal Black before he painted it Ruby Red, Pitch Black, Yellow, Oxford Blue and Creamy White. The fence was painted Jade Green before it was painted Pitch Black and Oxford Blue but was painted Jade Green after it was painted Navy Blue, Hazel Brown, Creamy White and Yellow. It was painted Yellow before it was painted Mauve but after it was painted Lavender.

My neighbour painted the fence Lavender before he painted it Coal Black, Ruby Red, Olive Green, Lemon, Pitch Black, Yellow and Mauve. He painted the fence Mauve after he painted it White but before he painted it Creamy White. In turn, he painted the fence Creamy White after he painted it Violet and after he painted it Sky Blue, but he painted it Sky Blue before he painted it Hazel Brown which was after he painted it Navy Blue, Olive green, Indigo and Violet.

The fence was painted Violet before it was Turquoise, Turquoise before it was Emerald Green, Emerald Green before it was Sky Blue, Sky Blue after it was Navy Blue, Navy Blue before it was Lavender, Lavender after it was Orange, Orange before it was Burgundy, and Burgundy before it was Navy Blue. He painted it Sea Blue before he painted it Purple which in turn was before he painted it Ruby Red and Primrose. The fence was painted Ruby Red before it was painted Red, and it was also painted Pitch Black and Oxford Blue before it was painted Red. He painted the fence Oxford Blue before painting it Ruby Red, Sea Blue, Purple and Primrose and painted it Primrose before painting it Ruby Red.

65

My neighbour painted his fence Orange before he painted it Oxford Blue, Violet and Navy Blue, but he painted it Navy Blue before he painted it Indigo and Violet, and Violet after he painted it Olive Green, Indigo and Burgundy. The fence was painted Fawn before it was painted Oxford Blue, but was painted Fawn after being painted Hazel Brown, Violet and Pitch Black.

The fence was painted Pitch Black before it was painted Sea Blue, Oxford Blue, Purple, Primrose and Ruby Red, but was painted Pitch Black after it was painted Hazel Brown which was before it was painted Oxford Blue and Coal Black. My neighbour painted the fence White before he painted it Emerald Green, Emerald Green after he painted it Lemon, and Lemon after he had painted it Olive Green, Turquoise and White, and White after he had painted it Violet but before he had painted it Turquoise, Coal Black and Oxford Blue. Also, the fence was painted Violet before it was painted Sky Blue, Burgundy before it was painted Indigo, and Indigo before it was painted Lavender.

Q94 Coin Puzzle* A101
Using twelve coins, create a square which has five coins along each side.

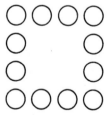

Q95 Grid Fill** H1, A134

Fit the 36 words into the grid below.

AXIAL   CLOTH   CURIO   DOMED   DRAMA   EGRET

ELOIN   ENACT   FIGHT   FORME   FRONT   GIANT

HODGE   HORDE   INFRA   IRADE   KNEEI   LARGE

LILAC   MOODY   NAMER   OFFAL   OIDIA   OLDIE

ORACH   ORATE   OSTIA   PATCH   PEDAL   RATEL

ROTOR   TEHEE   TIMER   TITLE   WAFER   WHELK

Q96 Square Cut* A78

Divide the square into four parts of equal size and shape,
each of which must include the letters A to P inclusive.

M	C	K	E	M	K	I	J
I	I	O	E	L	B	G	G
N	K	J	E	H	B	H	L
P	B	G	A	A	D	P	E
F	J	B	A	A	D	N	G
F	N	D	I	F	D	O	N
P	F	H	C	O	L	C	P
O	M	H	C	L	J	K	M

67

Q97 Roll The Die*   A68

Shown below is a die, resting on a corner square of a board divided into nine squares, forming a 3 × 3 grid. Opposite sides of the die total to seven so that the face on the opposite side of the face showing six spots only shows one spot; the face opposite the side showing two spots shows five spots; and the remaining face shows three spots. Given that you are only allowed to roll the die a quarter turn over a bottom edge so that it moves to an adjacent square (except diagonally), and you are only allowed to roll the die four or six times each turn, what number of spots, when the die is resting on the square in the position indicated by the dotted lines, never appears on the top face of the die?

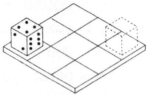

Q98 Number Fill**   A88

Given that the same number does not appear in two adjacent squares, either vertically, horizontally or diagonally, fit the numbers 1 to 15 inclusive four times each into the grid below. Only one number should be entered into each square. Some of the numbers appear next to the row and/or beneath the column into which they should be placed.

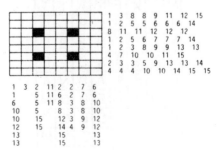

Q99   Cross Check*   A24

Look along each line horizontally, and then look down each line vertically, to find the missing square.

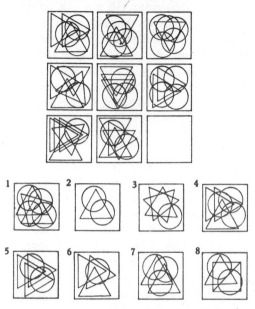

Q100   Logicalympics – Swimming**   H4, A48

Four countries entered the logicalympics swimming events: Great Britain (GB), the German Democratic Republic (GDR), the United States of America (USA) and the Union of Soviet Socialist Republics (USSR). There were eight events in all: 100m freestyle, 100m backstroke, 100m breaststroke, 100m butterfly, 200m freestyle, 200m back-stroke, 200m breaststroke and 200m butterfly. All four countries entered three swimmers in each of the eight events. In true logicalympic style, there was no overall winner; each of the four countries won two gold medals, two silver medals and two bronze medals. Given the follow-ing information, see if you can work out which country won

69

the gold medal, silver medal and bronze medal in each event.

The USA didn't win any 200m event and won no medals at all in any butterfly event. GB won one 100m event and one 200m event. USSR was the only country to win all three medals in one event. GDR won only one medal out of both butterfly events, and did not win a gold and silver medal in the same event. GB won a total of two medals in the breaststroke events. GDR won a silver medal in one of the breaststroke events and won a total of two medals in the back-stroke events. GB won a silver medal and a bronze medal in one of the 100m events. The USSR won a bronze medal in the 100m freestyle.

GB won only one bronze medal out of the four bronze medals for the 200m events, and did not win a silver medal in any of the 200m events. The USA won the bronze medal in both of the events where GB won the gold medal. The USSR won a silver medal in the 100m event won by GB which wasn't freestyle. The GDR won one 100m event and one 200m event. The USSR didn't win any medals in the 100m butterfly event. GB won one of the two 200m events in which the GDR won no medals at all. The USSR didn't win a single medal in any of the backstroke events. The GDR won a bronze medal and a silver medal in one of the 100m events.

Q101   What Next?*   A59
Find the next most appropriate pentagon.

Choose from:

70

Q102 Odd One Out* A113
Which one of the following ten diagrams is the odd one out?

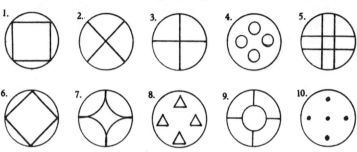

Q103 Logic Box* H6, A102
Using the information given below, place the letters A to P inclusive into the grid of 16 squares.

A is below I, which is to the left of C.
B is below O and to the left of C.
E is below H, which is to the left of A.
G is below F and to the left of B and C.
J is above M and to the right of H.
L is below K.
M is to the left of L.
N is above C and K.
O is to the left of D.
P is to the right of M.

('Above/below' refers to two letters in the same column.
'Left of/right of' refers to two letters in the same row.)

Q104 Clockwork Links*** H3, A124

Diagram One is that of the numbers 1, 2, 3 and 4, each of which is surrounded by eight squares, all of which contain a different letter. The eight letters in the squares around each number can be rotated around the number either 90° clockwise, 90° anticlockwise or 180°. For example, if the letters around the number 1 were rotated 90° clockwise, A would replace C, B would replace G, C would replace K, G would replace J, etc.

Diagram Two is that of Diagram One after eight rotations of the letters around the four numbers – three 90° clockwise, two 90° anticlockwise and three through 180°. The letters have been rotated twice around each number. In what order, and in which direction have the letters been rotated around each number to arrive at the positions shown in Diagram Two?

Diagram One

A	B	C	D	E
F	**1**	G	**2**	H
I	J	K	L	M
N	**3**	O	**4**	P
Q	R	S	T	U

Diagram Two

Q	D	A	N	K
F	**1**	R	**2**	L
E	H	M	B	C
J	**3**	G	**4**	T
I	P	U	O	S

Q105 Post Problem* A89

The diagram below represents a square courtyard containing nine wooden posts. I have two sets of fencing, each of which can form a square of any size. Using the two sets of fencing, is it possible to divide the courtyard into nine separate sections with one post in each section? If so, how?

Q106   Connection**   A142

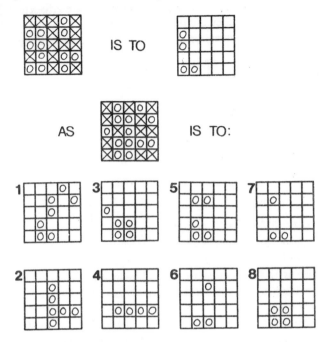

Q107   Patchy Problem**   A51

Shown below is a diagram representing a patchwork quilt consisting of 18 hexagonal-shaped patches. The quilt has been nailed to a blank white wall in five places, with the patches lettered A, E, H, L and O at the top. There are five red patches, five yellow patches, four green patches and four blue patches. No two adjacent patches are the same colour and no green patch has a nail through it. No patch which is adjacent to only four other patches is blue and no patch which is adjacent to only two other patches is green. Of the five vertical columns of patches, there is a yellow patch and a red patch in each column, no green patch in the second column from the left and no blue patch in the second column from the right. No blue patch is directly below a red patch, and each of the four patches which are adjacent to another six patches are different colours.

From the information given, what colour is each of the 18 patches?

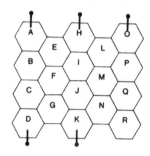

Q108 Blocked** H7, A7

Each of the 25 blocks of four letters shown below can be rotated about its centre, either 90° clockwise, 90° anticlockwise or 180°. When all of the 25 blocks are in their correct positions, all ten rows and columns contain the letters A to J only once.

Fourteen of the blocks shown below are not in their correct positions. Given that five blocks have been rotated clockwise and five blocks have been rotated anticlockwise, which 14 of the 25 have been rotated and in which direction?

	A	B	C	D	E
1	C J / B A	H J / G B	I D / E I	A G / D F	H C / F E
2	G F / C E	H F / D I	B C / A G	J I / B E	J A / H D
3	A I / D J	C I / F G	J C / H G	A H / B E	D F / B E
4	E H / I G	J E / B A	A D / F H	C D / F C	B I / G J
5	F H / D B	A E / C D	J B / E F	J H / I G	C G / A I

74

Q109 Say Cheese*** H8, A135

One of the local supermarkets has a special cheese counter where various types of cheese are all laid out in a straight line. The position of each type of cheese is never changed so that you can quickly select your choice of cheese when you visit the supermarket. From the following information, make a list of the cheeses in the order in which they are arranged on the supermarket counter, starting from the left-hand side and assuming you are facing the cheese counter.

The Stilton is to the left of the Mycella which is to the right of the Gruyère. The Gruyère is to the left of the Gambozola and Gloucester. The Gloucester is to the left of the Cottage which is to the right of the Gruyère. The Camembert is to the left of the Boursin which in turn is to the left of the Westminster Blue. The Westminster Blue is to the right of the Cottage as is the Boursin. The Gouda is to the left of the Brie which is to the right of the Gorgonzola. The Swiss is to the left of the Cotswold which in turn is to the left of the Lymeswold. The Lymeswold is to the left of the Gloucester and the Camembert. The Gorgonzola and the Gruyère are to the right of the Camembert.

The Tilsiter is to the left of the Pecorino which in turn is to the left of the Port Salut. The Port Salut is to the left of the Parmesan and the Wensleydale. The Wensleydale is to the left of the Gouda which is to the right of the Jarlsberg. The Jarlsberg is to the left of the Cheshire which in turn is to the left of the Swiss. The Swiss is to the right of the Port Salut which is to the left of the Camembert and the Brickbat. The Brickbat is to the left of the Swiss. The Roquefort is also to the left of the Swiss.

The Gorgonzola is to the left of the Wensleydale which is to the right of the Roquefort which in turn is to the left of the Cheshire. The Cheshire is to the left of the Brickbat which is to the right of the Parmesan. The Parmesan is to the left of the Jarlsberg which in turn is to the left of the Lymeswold. The Lymeswold is to the left of the Cottage which in turn is to the left of the Gambozola. The Gambozola is to the left of the Stilton which in turn is to the left of the Boursin and to the right of the Cottage.

The Cottage is to the left of the Mycella which in turn is to the left of the Boursin. The Boursin is to the right of the Port Salut as is the Gorgonzola. The Parmesan is to the left of the Lymeswold which is to the right of the Percorino which in turn is to the left of the Jarlsberg and to the right of the Edam. The Edam is to the left of the Tilsiter which in turn is to the left of the Brie. The Brie is to the left of the Gruyère which is to the right of the Port Salut.

The Port Salut is to the right of the Tilsiter and the Cheddar. The Cheddar is to the left of the Tilsiter. The Edam is to the left of the Jarlsberg and to the right of the Cheddar. The Cheddar is to the left of the Cottage. The Brie is also to the left of the Cottage. The Lymeswold is to the left of the Brie and the Gruyère which in turn is to the left of the Westminster Blue. The Brickbat and the Camembert are to the right of the Roquefort which is to the left of the Cottage.

The Cottage is to the right of the Camembert which is to the left of the Gouda. The Gouda is to the right of the Cotswold which in turn is to the right of the Tilsiter and the Jarlsberg. The Jarlsberg is to the left of the Gloucester and the Roquefort and is to the right of the Tilsiter and the Cheddar. The Tilsiter is to the left of the Lymeswold. The Stilton is to the right of the Gambozola and the Gruyère which in turn is to the left of the Boursin.

Complete the square so that all of the columns and rows contain the letters:

S Q U A R E B O X

Each of the nine letters must only appear once in each column or row.

B	S			Q				X
	E	X			B	R	O	
		Q	E	X			B	S
		A	X		E	U	B	
O	B			R				
X			A		S			O
		U		S		O		
	Q		O	E		S	U	
S		B			Q		X	A

Q111 Sparky** A69

Eddie the electrician has eight different jobs to complete today, all of which are at different times and at different houses in Bright Street. Eddie's secretary, who isn't organised at all, has left a list of jumbled notes about the jobs that have to be completed in Bright Street. Using these notes, see if you can construct a timetable for Eddie so that he knows which job needs completing at each house and the time he has to be there.

Notes

Mend dishwasher at No. 51. Mend fridge motor at 11.00am. Go to No. 31 at 4.00pm. You have a 10.00am appointment at Bright Street. Don't go to No. 13 first or

last. Go to No. 27 before installing cooker point at No. 14.
Install alcove light after mending dishwasher. Mend the
vacuum cleaner before the fridge motor. Your last job is at
5.00pm and your first at 9.00am. Mend the electric shower
at 3.00pm. Go to No. 2 before Nos. 14 and 9 and after 51.
Install the cooker point before mending the electric shower
but not after lunch. Do not mend the dishwasher first.
Mend the broken socket after the electric shower. Install
the wall lights at No. 43 after installing the alcove light at
No. 9. You have a 2.00pm and a 12noon appointment in
Bright Street.

Q112   Letter Boxes**   H5, A145

When the diagram below is complete, each column and row
should contain the letters A, B, C, D, E, F, G, H, I and J.
See if you can complete the diagram by fitting the seven
blocks of nine letters into the seven highlighted squares and
filling in the remaining squares.

A	J	F
D	I	A
J	E	G

E	B	C
J	D	B
G	C	H

E	D	A
I	E	D
C	J	F

F	H	B
G	C	I
D	G	H

G	D	I
E	B	J
I	A	B

A	J	I
E	A	F
D	B	A

D	F	H
H	G	I
E	I	J

Q113   Odd One Out*** A79

The diagrams below are that of a flattened cube and three views of the cube before it was flattened. Which of the three views is incorrect? This time only two of the dotted lines along which the original cube was folded are shown.

Q114   Odd Block Out** A103

Which is the odd block out?

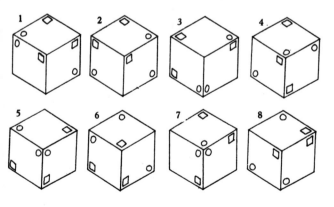

Q115 Logic Box* H6, A125

Using the information given below, place the letters A to P inclusive into the grid of 16 squares.

I is to the right of H and below B.
C is to the left of N and above H which is to the right of P.
P is below O and to the left of I.
M is below A which is also to the left of I.
K and F are to the right of L which is beiow G.
J is below D which is to the left of G and M.
E is above K and below B.

('Above/below' refers to two letters in the same column. 'Left of/right of' refers to two letters in the same row.)

Q116 What Next?* A114

What are the next three words in the following list? (Remember, there are no mathematics involved!)

one
seven
one
two
six
four
two
five
three
seven
four

_____
_____
_____

QII7 Nine By Four** A90
Complete the grid using the following information.

Each of the 36 squares in the grid is filled with a single-digit number from 1 to 9, each of those numbers being used four times. The same number must not appear in two touching squares, either across, down or diagonally. Column E does not contain a 4. Row one contains two 9s. Square B2 contains the number 8. Column F contains one 5, one 7 and one 8. Square F3 contains the number 1. Squares B3 and C5 contain the number 2. Column D does not contain two of any number. Square D2 contains the number 1. Column F contains two 3s. Row six contains three 5s, one 9 and one 7. Column C contains two 4s, one 6, one 1 and one 8. Square E5 contains the number 6. Row three contains one 5. Column D does not contain an 8 or a 9. Column A contains three 9s. Row two contains one 3, two 6s and two 8s. Column B does not contain two of any number. Row four contains two 1s, two 7s, one 6 and one 2.

```
     A   B   C   D   E   F
 1  _
 2
 3
 4
 5
 6
```

QII8 Chessboard* A18
Consider the following grid of letters.

                    Now, complete the grid below:

```
O U G R D          _ _ K _ _
T A L W I          _ _ _ B _
Y F Q C N          _ _ _ _ _
E K V H S          _ _ A _ _
J P B M X          N _ _ _ _
```

81

Q119 Block Cut* A29

Divide the rectangular block into four parts of equal size and shape. Each part should have the numbers 1 to 9 inclusive on the front, and all four new parts should form a square block when pieced together with all 36 numbers remaining the same way up.

```
1 2 8 6
5 4 3 9
7 6 5 7
8 9 4 1
1 3 8 2
2 7 9 3
4 5 6 1
8 3 7 4
6 2 9 5
```

Q120 Blocked** H7, A8

Each of the 25 blocks of four letters shown below can be rotated about its centre, either 90° clockwise, 90° anticlockwise or 180°. When all of the 25 blocks are in their correct positions, all ten rows and columns contain the letters A to J only once.

Sixteen of the blocks shown below are not in their correct positions. Which 16 of the 25 have been rotated and in which directions(s)?

	A	B	C	D	E
1	C D / B H	I H / A G	E G / J C	F B / D F	E I / A J
2	A E / I G	B G / C F	H J / F I	H E / A D	C B / D J
3	G I / A D	F D / B E	B E / C G	H J / J I	H F / A C
4	E F / F H	I J / J H	B A / A D	C G / G C	D E / I B
5	J B / C J	C D / E A	C D / H I	B A / I E	H G / G F

82

Q121   Grid Fill** H1, A35
Fit the 36 words into the grid below.

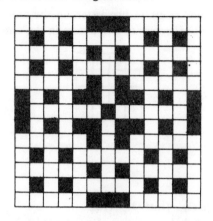

ABIDE	ADDLE	ADMIT	AFRIT	ALPHA	APHID
ASPIC	BENDY	CACHE	DENIM	EJECT	ELECT
ENACT	GUTSY	HADJI	HASTE	HEAVY	HEDGE
INTRO	LIVID	MITRE	NOMAD	PSALM	RAYED
RIANT	SCATT	SODIC	STUNG	TIPSY	TROUT
UDDER	UNMAN	UNRIP	URBAN	VICAR	YACHT

Q122   Logic Box* H6, A60
Using the information given below, place the letters A to P inclusive into the grid of 16 squares.

H is to the right of A which is to the left of N which is below B which is below L which is above C which is to the right of P which is to the right of J which is to the left of C which is to the right of F which is above K which is to the right of I which is above M which is below J which is below D which is to the left of O which is to the left of E which is above K

83

which is to the right of G which is above A which is below P
which is below O which is above G which is to the right of I.

('Above/below' refers to two letters in the same column.
'Left of/right of' refers to two letters in the same row.)

Q123   Odd One Out***   A104

The diagrams below are that of a flattened cube and three
views of the cube before it was flattened. Which of the three
views is incorrect? (This time only two of the dotted lines
along which the original cube was folded are shown.)

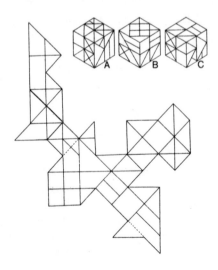

Q124 Clockwork Links*** H3, A136

Diagram One is that of the numbers 1, 2, 3 and 4, each of which is surrounded by eight squares, all of which contain a different letter. The eight letters in the squares around each number can be rotated around the number either 90° clockwise, 90° anticlockwise or 180°. For example, if the letters around the number 1 were rotated 90° clockwise, A would replace C, B would replace G, C would replace K, G would replace J, etc.

Diagram Two is that of Diagram One after eight rotations of the letters around the four numbers – three 90° clockwise, two 90° anticlockwise and three through 180°. The letters have been rotated twice around each number. In what order, and in which direction, have the letters been rotated around each number to arrive at the positions shown in Diagram Two?

Diagram One

A	B	C	D	E
F	**1**	G	**2**	H
I	J	K	L	M
N	**3**	O	**4**	P
Q	R	S	T	U

Diagram Two

K	N	Q	D	E
T	**1**	J	**2**	H
I	G	A	B	C
F	**3**	O	**4**	P
U	R	M	L	S

Q125 Odd One Out* A25

Which of the five numbered figures is the odd one out?

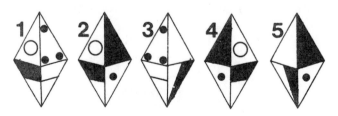

85

Q126 Connection** A49

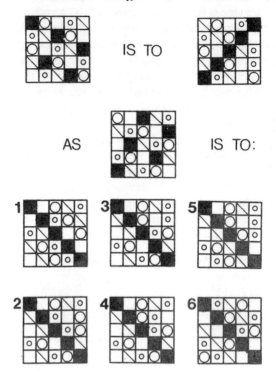

Q127 The Host* A70

A sat opposite G who was sitting next to C. C sat opposite F.
D sat between F and H, but not in seat 8 or 9. E sat between
G and A and opposite J. I sat between B and C but not in
seat 9. The host sat in seat 5. Who was the host?

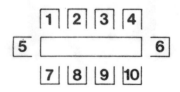

86

Q128 Logic Cube★★ H6, A80

Fit the 26 letters of the alphabet and the symbol '@' into the cube of 27 smaller cubes. Each letter is to be fitted into one of the smaller cubes, as is the '@'. Remember that some of the smaller cubes are not visible in the diagram below.

Y is behind R which is to the right of F. A is above T which in turn is above H. Y is in front of H. O is to the left of F and below B, which in turn is to the left of W. Q is behind N, E is behind V, P is behind @, J is behind Z, and I is behind L. S is above M and to the right of J, which in turn is above C. D is below L and to the right of N. W is above U, U is in front of M, and M is above P. V is to the left of @, G is to the left of X, and K is in front of S.

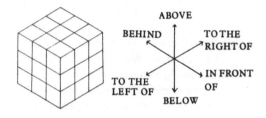

ABOVE

BEHIND ↑ TO THE RIGHT OF

TO THE LEFT OF ↓ IN FRONT OF

BELOW

Q129 Mix Up 16★★ H9, A115

Complete the grid so that all 16 columns and 16 rows contain the numbers 1 to 16 inclusive. When complete, the grid reads the same down as across.

1	2	3	4	5	6	7	8	9	10	11	12	13	14	15	16
2	6								4		11		3	16	12
3	9	12			5							16			7
4			15					11				16	1	14	3
5					13				16				11	15	
6	5	8	2	1			14		16	15			12	11	
7	10			15	2		16	3	14	11	6	9	8		
8	14			9			16	7			11	10	4		
9	8			1	16	15		13		5					10
10				16	6	2			15						14
11	15	4	8	12	16			9	6		10	~			1
12			16				3		1						5
13	7		16		10		1		14	8		2			9
14		16		9			12		7		15				13
15	16	13		7			7		5		3				2
16															

Q130   Advanced Academics***   A126

One afternoon, in the A Class of the Academy for Advanced Academics, the 25 students were given a seating plan for the next lecture, but there were no names allocated to the seats. Instead, there was a set of clues with the plan. Given the same seating plan and set of clues as the Advanced Academics, see if you can determine where each of the 25 students should sit during the next lecture.

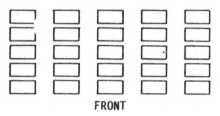

FRONT

Archy should sit behind Alred. Alroy should sit next to Askew. André, Aurel and Alred should sit in the same row. Alves should sit on Abram's right. Alwyn should sit in one of the four corner seats. Allan and Aaron should sit in the same row. Anson should sit on Abner's right. André should sit in front of Alwin and Aubyn. Alban should sit on Abram's left. Aaron should sit in front of Ariel, Alves and Abner. Alban should sit in front of Alwyn. Airay should sit behind Angus and Alroy. Abdul should sit behind Aubyn. Algie should not sit in the front row. Anson should sit in the same row as Alwin. Athol should sit in front of Anson. André should sit in one of the four corners. Alban should sit in front of Anton. Aaron should sit behind Askew. Aubyn should sit on Airay's right. Allan should sit between Aaron and Archy. Algie should not sit in the back row. Amand should not sit in the same row as Allan.

('Sit behind' or 'sit in front of' means in the same column, but not necessarily next to each other. All of the students should sit facing the front of the class.)

Q131   Birthday Boys**   H4, A19

Eddie has bought a video cassette tape, a compact disc, a cassette tape and a record token as presents for his brothers' birthdays, all of which are next week. Given the following information, what will each brother get?

Alan will not get the compact disc unless Barry gets the video cassette tape and David gets the cassette tape. Barry will not get the cassette tape unless Carl gets the record token and Alan gets the video cassette tape. David will not get the record token unless Alan gets the compact disc and Barry gets the video cassette tape. Alan will not get the video cassette tape unless Carl gets the record token and David gets the cassette tape. Barry will not get the video cassette tape unless Alan gets the record token and David gets the cassette tape. Alan will not get the record token unless Barry gets the compact disc and Carl gets the video cassette tape. Carl will not get the record token unless Barry gets the compact disc and Alan gets the cassette tape. Alan will not get the cassette tape unless Barry gets the record token and David gets the compact disc. Carl will not get the video cassette tape unless David gets the compact disc.

Q132   Combination*   A91

The diagram below represents a dial on a safe which has 12 points, one of them black. The black point, presently pointing toward a black dot, is to be turned to each letter in turn, but not in alphabetical order, to open the safe. The dial should be turned toward the letters as follows.

A before D but after B. B before C but after H. H before F, F before G, G before I and I before J. H after K, K before F, F after D, D before G, and G after E. E before D, C before

E, E after B, C before G, and A after E.

What is the order of letters to which the black point should be turned in order to open the safe?

Q133 Odd One Out*** A105

The diagrams below are that of a flattened cube and three views of the cube before it was flattened. Which of the three views is incorrect? (This time only two of the dotted lines along which the original cube was folded are shown.)

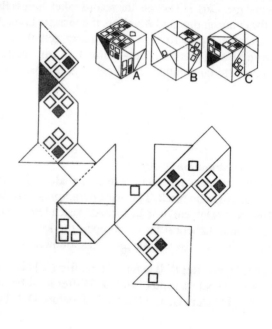

Q134 Logic Cube** H6, A116

Fit the 26 letters of the alphabet and the symbol '@' into the cube of 27 smaller cubes. Each letter is to be fitted into one of the smaller cubes, as is the '@'. Remember that some of the smaller cubes are not visible in the diagram below.

H is below C which is below D. I is to the right of S, S is to the right of M, and M is below A, which in turn is to the left of J. X is below J and in front of V which is above Y. E is in front of Y and to the right of L. H is behind @ and I is in front of @. W is in front of G which is above V and to the right of Z. Z is behind U and above P. R is behind L. N is in front of O and above B. B is to the right of F which is in front of J. Q is to the right of K.

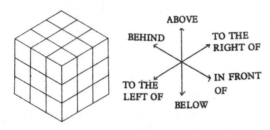

Q135 Which Way Next?* A41

The 10 × 10 grid of squares originally contained 98 squares containing an arrow, one square containing one dot, and one square containing two dots. The arrows pointed in eight different directions as shown in the eight numbered squares to the right of the grid. If you started at the square containing one dot and move to one of the three adjacent squares, then moved to the next adjacent square indicated by the arrow in the square you were on, and continued to do so, you would eventually land on the square containing two dots; and at the same time would have already landed on each and every square in the grid. The arrows have since been replaced by letters, the same letter being used to replace the same type of arrow throughout the grid. See if you can work out which letter replaced each of the eight types of arrow.

A	A	A	D	B	E	E	A	A	••
C	B	E	E	F	H	D	A	G	B
F	G	F	E	H	H	F	D	G	C
F	C	O	C	H	H	B	F	A	C
D	C	H	H	O	B	G	F	A	G
H	A	F	G	C	O	O	G	F	G
C	E	D	C	D	B	C	H	B	C
H	B	H	H	O	C	O	B	A	C
C	H	G	B	E	H	B	B	F	G
•	H	E	H	E	E	A	H	A	C

↑ 1 ↗ 2 → 3 ↘ 4 ↓ 5 ↙ 6 ← 7 ↖ 8

Q136 Blocked*** H7, A137

Each of the 25 blocks shown below has been rotated about its centre, either 90° clockwise or 90° anticlockwise. When all of the 25 blocks are in their correct positions, all ten rows and columns contain the letters A to J only once. In which direction has each of the 25 blocks been rotated?

	A	B	C	D	E
1	E D / I J	D E / A B	F A / B G	C H / H J	C F / G I
2	G C / O E	I J / J H	O F / G C	E A / B F	I B / A H
3	F G / J H	F B / O E	H I / I J	C O / A G	C B / A E
4	B C / I B	A C / H F	A J / D E	F G / I E	J D / H G
5	A F / H A	G C / I G	C E / H B	D J / B I	E F / J D

92

Q137 Letter Boxes** H5, A9

When the diagram below is complete, each column and row should contain the letters A, B, C, D, E, F, G, H, I and J. See if you can complete the diagram by fitting the eight blocks of nine squares into the eight highlighted squares in the diagram, and then filling in the remaining squares in the diagram and the eight blocks.

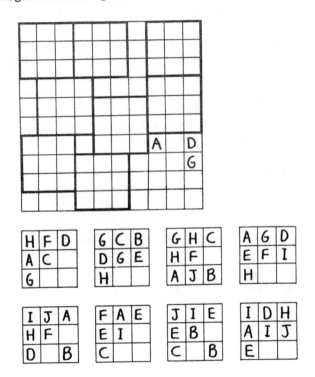

Q138 Clockwork Links*** H3, A61

Diagram One is that of the numbers 1, 2, 3 and 4, each of which is surrounded by eight squares, all of which contain a different letter. The eight letters in the squares around each number can be rotated around the number either 90° clockwise, 90° anticlockwise or 180°. For example, if the letters around the number 1 were rotated 90° clockwise, A would replace C, B would replace G, C would replace K, G would replace J, etc.

Diagram Two is that of Diagram One after eight rotations of the letters around the four numbers – three 90° clockwise, two 90° anticlockwise and three through 180°. The letters have been rotated twice around each number. In what order, and in which direction, have the letters been rotated around each number to arrive at the positions shown in Diagram Two?

Diagram One

A	B	C	D	E
F	**1**	G	**2**	H
I	J	K	L	M
N	**3**	O	**4**	P
Q	R	S	T	U

Diagram Two

A	R	G	Q	E
K	**1**	J	**2**	N
C	L	O	T	H
O	**3**	U	**4**	P
B	M	I	S	F

Q139 What Next?** A30

Which of the four lettered figures is next in the numbered sequence?

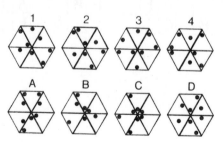

Q140 Logic Cube** H6, A106

Fit the 26 letters of the alphabet and the symbol '@' into the cube of 27 smaller cubes. Each letter is to be fitted into one of the smaller cubes, as is the '@'. Remember that some of the smaller cubes are not visible in the diagram below.

V is above H which is in front of S which is above E which is behind F which is to the right of M which is in front of X. A is above G which is above O which is behind I which is behind L which is to the right of Z which is to the right of R which is below J which is to the left of V. P is behind C which is to the left of U which is below N which is in front of D. K is above @, behind Q and to the left of Y which is above S. B is to the left of W and T is in front of Y.

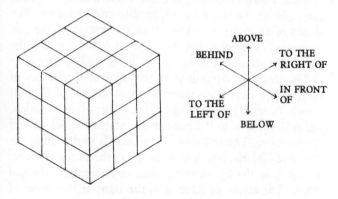

ABOVE

BEHIND

TO THE
RIGHT OF

IN FRONT
OF

TO THE
LEFT OF

BELOW

Q141 Temple Teaser*** H8, A117

Recent excavations at a temple in Greece unearthed a wall in which there were a line of recesses. In each recess was a statue of a Greek goddess. Given the following jumbled-up information, list the names of the statues from right to left.

The statue of Iris is to the left of the statues of Nemesis, Pleiades, Hebe, Rhea, Nike, Ate and Moirai. The statue of Moirai is to the right of the statues of Ate and Hebe. The statue of Hebe is to the left of the statue of Ate which in turn is to the right of the statue of Amphitrite. The statue of Amphitrite is to the left of the statues of Iris, Terpsichore, Hebe and Hygiea. The statue of Hygiea is to the left of the statue of Chloris which is to the left of the statue of Iris which is to the right of the statue of Artemis which is to the left of the statues of Hebe, Amphitrite, Chloris and Pleiades.

The statues of Pleiades, Hestia, Hygiea, Selene, Eos and Artemis are all to the right of the statue of Hera which in turn is to the right of the statues of Aphrodite, Athene, Demeter, Hecate and Irene. The statue of Irene is to the left of the statues of Artemis and Persephone. The statue of Persephone is to the left of the statues of Amphitrite, Ate, Athene, Danae, Iris, Terpsichore, Tyche and Opis, and to the right of the statues of Aphrodite and Demeter. The statue of Demeter is to the left of the statues of Hecate, Hebe and Aphrodite, but the statue of Aphrodite is to the left of the statues of Irene, Eos, Chloris and Artemis.

The statue of Artemis is to the right of the statues of Athene and Eos, Eos's statue being to the left of Hygiea, which, in turn, is to the right of the statue of Opis, which, again in turn, is to the right of the statues of Selene and Terpsichore. The statue of Terpsichore is to the left of the statue of Chloris, which is to the left of the statue of Hebe, which is to the left of the statues of Nemesis, Nike and Rhea. The statue of Rhea is to the right of the statue of Nemesis and to the left of the statues of Ate and Nike. The statue of Nike is to the left of the statue of Ate. The statue of Danae is to the right of the statues of Athene, Hestia and Selene.

The statue of Selene is to the left of the statues of Hestia, Amphitrite and Hebe. The statue of Hebe is to the right of the statue of Pleiades, the statue of Hecate is to the left of the statues of Irene and Aphrodite, and the statue of Eos is to the right of the statue of Tyche. Finally, the statue of Tyche is to the right of the statues of Danae and Hestia.

Q142 Laser Maze*** H2, A81

The diagram below represents an aerial view of a room which has been divided into 100 squares, as shown by the dotted lines. In each of the squares there should be a dot marked on the floor in the centre of the square, or a double-sided mirror. When all of the dots and mirrors are in their correct places, a laser beam can enter the room at square A1 in the direction indicated by an arrow, and leave the room from square J10. At the same time, the laser beam shines over each and every dot marked on the floor. When the beam reaches a mirror it 'bounces off' at an angle of 90°, but it never crosses itself. If the beam hits the outside wall it is absorbed by the wall and can go no further.

Twenty of the dots/mirrors are not in place; eight dots (X), seven mirrors from lower left to upper right (Y), and five mirrors from upper left to lower right (Z). See if you can determine which of the squares containing '?' should be replaced by:

1. X squares;   2. Y squares;   3. Z squares.

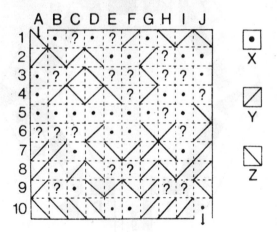

97

A does not live at numbers 1 or 17. F lives directly opposite
B, K lives directly opposite N, and M lives directly opposite
H. E does not live at numbers 5 or 7 but does live directly
opposite P. C, N and G live in the same block of three
houses as do B, J and P. The block in which B, J and P live is
not the first block of houses you pass by if you walk clockwise past the houses. O lives directly opposite J, D lives
directly opposite G, and Q lives directly opposite C. K, J
and O each live in one of the houses which are in the centre
of a block of three. L does not live in a block of three houses.
P does not live at numbers 8 or 9, C does not live at 12 or 13,
and I does not live at 9, 16 or 17. M lives in a house which is
part of a block of three. If walking past the houses clockwise, the path to D's house is the path after the path to L's
house, and you would arrive at B's house before J's.

  Who lives in each of the 17 houses?

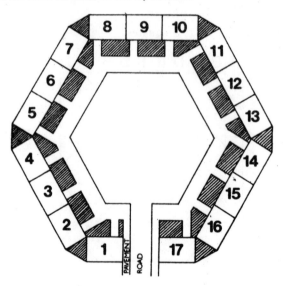

Just after the detectives working on the case of 'Who killed Lord Logic?' had completed their statements, all of the lights went out and there was a very loud scream. Two minutes later, the lights went back on again and Lady Logic was found lying dead in the hallway. There was quite a lot of blood on the floor and it looked as if her body had been dragged from either the kitchen or the dining room. The detective in charge called upon another two detectives who had just arrived at Logic Manor to help in solving this latest possible murder. A gun, a knife, a rope and a crowbar were found lying in the corner of the hallway. There were three people who could have murdered Lady Logic, all of whom were each interviewed by all seven detectives. Given the three people who could have murdered Lady Logic, a list of all 21 statements given to the seven detectives, and the fact that only seven of the 21 statements are true, who did it, where and with what?

Detective	Suspect	Statement given by suspect
1	Maid	I did not kill Lady Logic in the kitchen using a gun.
2	Maid	I did not kill Lady Logic in the dining room with a knife.
3	Maid	The butler did it with a rope in the kitchen.
4	Maid	The butler did not do it using a crowbar in the kitchen.
5	Maid	The butler shot Lady Logic.
6	Maid	The mistress did not kill Lady Logic in the kitchen.
7	Maid	The mistress used the gun to kill Lady Logic.

1	Butler	I murdered Lady Logic by stabbing her with a knife.
2	Butler	The maid used a gun to murder Lady Logic.
3	Butler	The mistress used a crowbar to kill Lady Logic.
4	Butler	The maid did not kill Lady Logic in the dining room.
5	Butler	The mistress used a rope to kill Lady Logic in the kitchen.
6	Butler	The maid used a knife to stab Lady Logic to death in the dining room.
7	Butler	The maid used a rope to hang Lady Logic in the dining room.
1	Mistress	The maid shot Lady Logic in the dining room.
2	Mistress	The butler hit Lady Logic over the head with a crowbar.
3	Mistress	The butler stabbed Lady Logic with a knife in the kitchen.
4	Mistress	The maid killed Lady Logic in the dining room with a crowbar.
5	Mistress	The maid killed Lady Logic using a knife in the dining room.
6	Mistress	I killed Lady Logic in the kitchen using a rope.
7	Mistress	I killed Lady Logic in the kitchen using a knife.

Q145 Odd One Out*** A62

The diagrams below are that of a flattened cube and three views of the cube before it was flattened. Which of the three views is incorrect? (This time only two of the dotted lines along which the original cube was folded are shown.)

Q146 3D Movement*** A20

The diagram below is that of a large cube divided into 27 smaller cubes. I know that, if I start in the centre of the smaller cube indicated by the arrow and move in the following directions in the following order, I will finish in the centre of one of the four lettered cubes: right, down, left, down, forward, up, right, backwards, left, down, right, up, forward, down, backwards, left, forward and up. But I don't know if I have to move a distance of one or two cubes each time. One thing I do know is that I must pass through the centre of all 27 cubes only once. See if you can work out the distance I must move in each of the 19 directions.

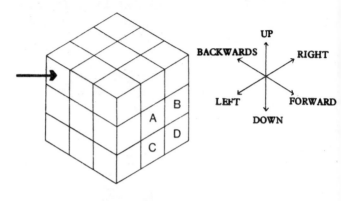

Q147 Grid Fill – Numbers*** A71
Fit the 36 numbers into the grid below.

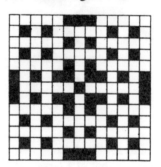

07492	14679	14793	14987	18671	18962
23149	24693	26794	29183	35444	36794
41397	46578	49234	51709	56676	61341
63927	64139	64328	65896	67532	71934
73421	74321	75269	78261	78549	81432
84652	85679	89765	98532	98653	99289

Q148 Logicalympics – The Beginning*** H4, A36

Although there are never any winners or losers at the Logicalympics, there is one time during the whole event where the countries are in order one after another. This is at the opening ceremony when all of the participating teams enter the stadium with the team captain carrying their flag. Given the following information, in what order did the teams enter the stadium?

The Australian team entered the stadium before the team from Norway and after the teams from Turkey and Finland, both of which entered the stadium before the teams from Algeria, the German Democratic Republic and Yugoslavia. Denmark's team entered the stadium after the teams from Algeria, Japan, Portugal, USSR and Venezuela. The team from Venezuela entered the stadium before the team from USSR and after the teams for Portugal and Japan. Both of the teams from Portugal and Japan entered the stadium before the teams from USA, Sweden and USSR.

The team from Turkey entered the stadium before the team from Portugal, and the team from Greece entered the stadium before the team from Japan, but the teams from Algeria and Canada entered the stadium before both Portugal's team and the team from Japan. Japan's team entered the stadium after the teams from France, Hungary, Portugal and Finland. The team from Romania entered the stadium before the teams from Mexico, Norway, Greece, Finland, India and Canada, and the team from Canada entered the stadium before the teams from Algeria, France and Greece, but after the teams from Brazil, Great Britain, India and Spain. The team from Spain entered the stadium before the teams from Turkey and Romania both of which entered the stadium after the teams from Brazil and Hungary.

The team from Hungary entered the stadium before the

103

teams from Austria and Brazil, the latter of which entered the stadium after the team from Austria but before the teams from Spain, India and France. The team from France entered the stadium before the team from Portugal who in turn entered before the team from Greece. The team from the German Democratic Republic entered the stadium after the teams from Great Britain and Mexico, but before the team from Yugoslavia. The team from Mexico also entered the stadium before the team from Yugoslavia.

The team from Algeria entered the stadium before the teams from New Zealand and Norway, as did the team from India. The teams from Denmark, Great Britain and New Zealand entered the stadium after the team from Turkey. The team from France entered the stadium after the teams from Norway and New Zealand and the team from New Zealand entered the stadium before the team from Australia. The team from Romania entered the stadium after the teams from Great Britain and Austria, the latter of which entered the stadium before the team from Spain. The team from Sweden entered the stadium before the team from Venezuela which in turn entered the stadium before the team from USSR. The team from Mexico entered the stadium after the team from Finland, and the team from Yugoslavia entered the stadium before the team from India.

When the grid below is complete, it contains the numbers 1 to 20 inclusive, 20 times each. Given that no column or row contains the same number more than once, see if you can fill in the missing numbers.

1	2	3	4	5	6	7	8	9	10	11	12	13	14	15	16	17	18	19	20
2	18	1		3			14		12				19					4	
3				16		15	1					6	17	5	8		2	14	
4			11				7	8				16		1	2	18		20	
5	15		11			9	2			16	4			14	13		8		
6		5				3	19	16	13	15		12		20					
7	10				1	15					14			12	17	4	5	9	16
8		17	5	9		2		16	19	7			18	4		15	10	6	
9	11	10	19		15	14	16	17		2	4	5		6				.	13
10		20		12	19	16	6		18	9		15		17	1	2		11	
11			10	6	17	13	7	3			2	14	8			16	4		9
12	5	11	20	17			13		2	16	1			7		15	10	6	
13	17	14	9		2				20		12		11	5		3			
14	13	16	15	10	9		11		5	8	7			20			18	19	
15					9	10				3	4	14	13	19	20	17	18		
16		15		2			6	18	5		20	10	11	12	13	1	8		
17	12	9	3		5		18		4	1	19		13			11	7		
18			2		8	10	19		1	15	20		3	13				16	4
19	9	.7		1	11	5	20	8			17		16	2	12				
20	7		16		10	11	17	5	15	14			2	3		8	12		

Q150 3D Logic*** A10

DIAGRAM (A)   DIAGRAM (B)

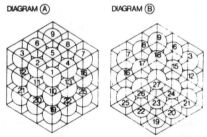

Diagram A is that of a view of a cube from above. Diagram B is that of the same cube from below and behind. The cube consists of a wire framework which also divides the cube into 27 smaller cubes. In each of the 27 smaller cubes there is a sphere which is large enough to touch the sphere in any vertically or horizontally adjacent cube. Also, the spheres have been numbered from 1 to 27, the centre sphere being number 14. The spheres have also been allocated a letter of the alphabet or an '@' symbol, all 27 of them being different. Given the following information, see if you can determine which letter or '@' symbol has been allocated to each of the 27 spheres.

Sphere I does not touch sphere L, sphere A does not touch spheres N, D or M, sphere K does not touch spheres T or U, and sphere W does not touch sphere U. Sphere B does not touch either sphere C or sphere H but is directly above sphere Y. Sphere F is not directly above or directly below spheres S or I. Sphere @ does not touch sphere J and sphere O does not touch sphere P. Spheres L and N are directly above sphere @. Sphere 20 has been allocated the letter E. The top layer consists of the spheres numbered 1 to 9 inclusive, the bottom layer consists of the spheres numbered 19 to 27 inclusive, and the remaining spheres form the middle layer.

Spheres A, B and C are not in the bottom layer. Spheres B and E are not in the same or adjacent layers, neither are C and F, X and V, S and E, Z and Q, R and J, B and P, F and H, J and B, and I and @. Spheres D, E, F and G are not in the top layer, nor do any of them touch each other. Spheres M, N, O and P are not in the top layer. Sphere Q is in the layer below the layer containing sphere M. Spheres @, L, Y, Q and O touch only three other spheres each. Spheres F and @ touch each other.

Sphere R is directly above sphere O. Sphere V is not in the top layer and touches five other spheres. Spheres E and @ do not touch each other. Sphere X touches five other spheres. Spheres E and O touch each other. Sphere C is not numbered 4 or 6. Spheres S and I are not numbered 2 or 4. Sphere Z is directly above sphere U. Sphere T touches only four other spheres. Sphere G does not touch spheres D, U or N, but is directly above sphere V. If a sphere is directly above another sphere they are not always touching; for example, sphere 1 is directly above sphere 19.

Hints

1. There are four squares consisting of four words each. Start by constructing these four squares. The two words starting in the top left-hand corner share the same first letter, therefore words with no first letter the same as any other word can be eliminated, as can words whose middle letter or last letter do not appear as the first letter of any of the other words. Then, fill in the words across each of the four squares. Once you have completed the four squares, consider the possibility of each square in each of the four positions, eliminating the impossible positions due to lack of connecting words.

2. Start by eliminating the part-answers which do not work. For example, if a Y mirror were to be placed in square A4 in Q7, then the laser beam would go no further; or if a dot X were placed in the same square the laser beam would then 'bounce off' the mirrors in A5, B5 and then B3 and end up being absorbed by the wall in square A3, leaving A4 to be filled by a Z mirror. Continue through the maze in a similar fashion, but if you get stuck try working backwards or on a particular square or squares.

3. Start with the letters furthest away from their original position and then work backwards.

4. Work out all the possibilities, then read through the information/clues, eliminating each impossible combination until you are left with the correct one. Often the information/clues need to be read more than once or twice.

5. Start by checking where each of the blocks cannot possibly fit. For example in Q9, the block to the right of the grid does not fit in the top left-hand highlighted square, as it would result in the letter F occurring twice in the third column from the left. Then, cross-check the blocks with each other vertically and horizontally so that you

know which blocks do not fit or overlap in the same column or row.

6. Consider the possibility of each letter being in every square/cube, then read the clues/information through and eliminate the letters which cannot be in each square/cube, leaving only the correct letter in each square/cube. Often the clues/information will have to be read through more than once, each time revealing a part of the full solution.

7. Start by checking which letters there are none of, or more than one of, in each column and row. Then, first consider rotating the blocks containing the excess or lack of the aforementioned letters. Also, keep count of the number of blocks rotated in each column/row and the direction in which they have been rotated, rather than trying to decide in which direction a block has been rotated when there are only one or two possibilities left.

8. Carefully read the information given and then list all of the different subjects or objects, unless they are already listed for you. Then, either consider the possibility of each one being in all of the different positions/places, and eliminate each incorrect part or full solution by reading and/or re-reading the information/clues given; or list and re-list the objects/subjects each time you read the information/clues until the solution is correct and matches all of the information/clues correctly.

9. In the first column of Q46, the letters R and U are missing. U cannot fit in the 5th row as there is already a letter U in that row. Therefore the letter U must fit in row 6 and the letter R in row 5. Continue this process until the grid is complete, not necessarily completing one complete column or row at a time.

Solutions

A1 Odd One Out Q15
Cube C.

A2 Blocked Q30
Blocks rotated anticlockwise = A1, A3, B3, B5, C1, D2, D3, E5;
Blocks rotated clockwise = A5, B2, C2, C4, D4, E1, E4.

A3 Mix Up Square Q46

A4 Odd One Out Q61
A.

A5 Grid Fill Q75
The words can also be fitted into the grid in a mirror image
(diagonally) of the solution shown below.

A6 Laser Maze Q90
1. X squares = B3, G10, I7;
2. Y squares = A8, B1, C8, D1, H3;
3. Z squares = A7, C1, C5, C7, F8, G3, H2, J5.

A7 Blocked Q108
Blocks rotated anticlockwise = A1, B2, C4, D3, E5;
Blocks rotated clockwise = A4, B5, C1, D2, E3;
Blocks rotated 180° = A3, C3, D5, E1.

A8 Blocked Q120
Blocks rotated anticlockwise = A1, A2, A3, C3, D1;
Blocks rotated clockwise = B2, B3, C4, D2, D5;
Blocks rotated 180° = B4, C5, D3, E1, E4, E5.

A9 Letter Boxes Q137

H	F	D	G	C	B	E	I	J	A
A	C	I	D	G	E	B	H	F	J
G	J	C	H	F	I	A	D	E	B
I	G	H	C	B	D	J	F	A	E
B	H	F	J	A	G	D	E	I	C
D	A	J	B	E	F	I	C	G	H
J	I	E	F	H	C	G	A	B	D
E	B	A	I	D	H	F	J	C	G
C	E	B	A	I	J	H	G	D	F
F	D	G	E	J	A	C	B	H	I

A10 3D Logic Q150

1 = Z	10 = U	19 = Q
2 = C	11 = A	20 = E
3 = R	12 = T	21 = O
4 = H	13 = M	22 = F
5 = X	14 = G	23 = V
6 = I	15 = W	24 = J
7 = L	16 = N	25 = @
8 = S	17 = K	26 = P
9 = B	18 = D	27 = Y

A11 Grid Fill Q4

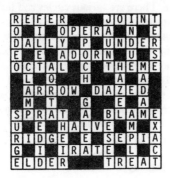

A12 The Mad Hatter Q26

The Mad Hatter wore the top hat on Friday and the fez is orange.
The full solution is as follows:

Monday –	Stetson –	Blue
Tuesday –	Bowler hat –	Red
Wednesday –	Trilby –	Green
Thursday –	Cap –	Yellow
Friday –	Top hat –	White
Saturday –	Fez –	Orange
Sunday –	Sombrero –	Black

A13 Double Wordsquare Q37

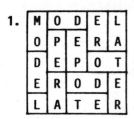
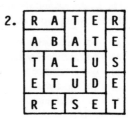

A14 What Next? Q56

B is the next most appropriate square.
Each square is divided into four smaller squares of equal size. In

the centre of each of these smaller squares is another square which does not change. There are various circles and lines surrounding each of these squares that don't change, which, as the sequence progresses, rotate around the square in a clockwise direction. The various lines and circles rotate at different speeds. They rotate twice the distance in the upper right-hand square as they do in the upper left-hand square, and twice the distance in the lower right-hand square as they do in the upper right-hand square. Finally, they rotate twice the distance in the lower left-hand square as they do in the lower right-hand square.

A15 Number Fill Q71

12	10	1	8	3	1	3
7	2	7	12	7	10	7
4	10	5	9	3	1	3
11	2	8		11	5	6
4	5	9	12	2	9	11
12	10	2	5	8	1	6
4	6	8	11	6	9	4

A16 Clockwork Q88
The letters around the numbers given in brackets were rotated in the following order and direction:

(4) – 90° anticlockwise;
(3) – 90° anticlockwise;
(2) – 90° clockwise;
(1) – 90° clockwise;
(2) – 90° clockwise;
(3) – 180°;
(4) – 90° anticlockwise.

A17 Odd One Out Q92
C.

A18 Chessboard Q118

Each letter has been moved one square to the right and two squares down. Where the letter would move off the grid, the grid has been treated as continuous.

S	E	K	V	H
X	J	P	B	M
D	O	U	G	R
I	T	A	L	W
N	Y	F	Q	C

A19 Birthday Boys Q131

Alan—cassette tape;
Barry—record token;
Carl—video cassette tape;
David—compact disc.

A20 3D Movement Q146

Direction	Distance in cubes
Right	Two
Down	One
Left	Two
Down	One
Forward	Two
Up	Two
Right	One
Backwards	One
Left	One
Down	One
Right	Two
Up	One
Forward	One
Down	Two
Backwards	Two
Left	One
Forward	Two
Up	One

113

A21 Logic Box Q10

```
H C A
B G E
F I D
```

A22 Logic Box Q39

```
E I B
A G D
H C F
```

A23 Clockwork Q70

The letters around the numbers given in brackets were rotated in the following order and direction:

(1) – 180°;
(2) – 180°;
(4) – 90° anticlockwise;
(3) – 180°;
(2) – 90° anticlockwise;
(3) – 90° clockwise;
(4) – 90° clockwise.

The third rotation shown above could take place first without any effect on the outcome, as there is no further effect until the fourth rotation which then alters the positions of the letters moved by the first three rotations.

A24 Cross Check Q99

Number 4. The number of triangles increase by one vertically and decrease by one horizontally. The circles increase by one horizontally and decrease by one vertically.

A25 Odd One Out Q125

Number 2 is the odd one out. The remaining four figures are all different views of the same solid figure. (Two 'pyramids' attached at the base.)

114

A26 Auntie Christmas   Q29

Auntie Carol will get the slippers. (Auntie Sheila will get the voucher, Auntie Mary the chocolates and Auntie Joan the flowers.)

A27 Letter Boxes   Q59

F	H	J	G	D	C	I	A	B	E
G	C	B	D	A	H	E	I	F	J
B	I	D	H	E	J	A	G	C	F
E	D	I	A	F	G	J	B	H	C
D	A	C	F	H	B	G	E	J	I
C	E	H	J	B	A	F	D	I	G
J	F	A	I	G	E	C	H	D	B
H	J	F	E	I	D	B	C	G	A
I	G	E	B	C	F	D	J	A	H
A	B	G	C	J	I	H	F	E	D

A28 Logic Box   Q86

I	B	P	E
O	F	A	N
C	L	G	K
H	J	M	D

A29 Block Cut   Q119

A30 What Next?   Q139

B. The hexagon is divided into three pairs of triangles. Firstly, at each stage, the hexagon rotates 60° clockwise about its centre. Secondly, a change takes place in the position of the dots in the pairs of triangles at each stage.

1. Pair one – the two triangles containing two dots each. The dots appear in two corners of the triangles with the empty corner moving in a clockwise direction in one triangle and an anticlockwise direction in the other triangle.

2. Pair two – one pair of triangles containing a single dot each. They start with one dot in the centre of the face common with the hexagon and a dot in the corner of the triangle nearest the centre of the hexagon. Each dot moves in the following sequence; outside edge, centre, and centre corner of the triangle. One step being taken each rotation of the hexagon. Both dots only being in the same position of the sequence when they are in the centre of their respective triangles.

3. Pair three – the remaining two triangles. The dots in the triangles move clockwise in one triangle and anticlockwise in the other triangle. Both move one half the distance of one side of the triangle each time the hexagon rotates 60°.

A31 Paint by Numbers Q1
Sections 5 and 7.

A32 Square Cut Q31

A33 Wordsquares Q62
1. HOME   2. LIMP   3. DOTE   4. TEAM
    OPEN   IDEA   ORAL   EDGE
    MEMO   MEAL   TASS   AGAR
    ENOW   PALE   ELSE   MERE

A34 Father Unlike Son Q91
Plumber.

A35 Grid Fill Q121

The words can also be fitted into the grid in a mirror image (diagonally) of the solution shown below.

A36 Logicalympics – The Beginning Q148

The teams entered the stadium in the following order:

1. Hungary
2. Austria
3. Brazil
4. Spain
5. Turkey
6. Great Britain
7. Romania
8. Finland
9. Mexico
10. German Democratic Republic
11. Yugoslavia
12. India
13. Canada
14. Algeria
15. New Zealand
16. Australia
17. Norway
18. France
19. Portugal
20. Greece
21. Japan
22. Sweden
23. Venezuela
24. USSR
25. Denmark
26. USA

A37 Odd Block Out Q18

4. The remaining seven blocks are all different views of the same block.

A38 Grid Fill Q48

The words can also be fitted into the grid in a mirror image (diagonally) of the solution below.

A39 Gruffs Q78

1. Retriever
2. Bull Terrier
3. Whippet
4. Great Dane
5. Chow
6. Bulldog
7. Yorkshire Terrier
8. King Charles Spaniel
9. Greyhound
10. Chihuahua
11. Dachshund
12. Spaniel
13. Dalmatian
14. Afghan Hound
15. Beagle
16. Bull Mastiff
17. Foxhound
18. Labrador
19. Poodle
20. Collie
21. Pug
22. St Bernard
23. Griffon
24. Sheepdog
25. Alsatian
26. Dobermann Pinscher.

A40 Mix Up Squarebox Q110

B	S	O	U	Q	R	A	E	X
U	E	X	S	A	B	R	O	Q
R	A	Q	E	X	O	B	S	U
Q	R	A	X	O	E	U	B	S
O	B	S	Q	R	U	X	A	E
X	U	E	A	B	S	Q	R	O
E	X	U	B	S	A	O	Q	R
A	Q	R	O	E	X	S	U	B
S	O	B	R	U	Q	E	X	A

A41   Which Way Next?   Q135

C = 1; H = 2; A = 3; D = 4; F = 5; B = 6; E = 7; G = 8.

There is a quick way of solving the puzzle rather than trying each different type of arrow in place of each letter. You must always stay in the grid boundary, therefore if any of the letters in the top row replaced arrows numbered 1, 2 or 8 this would not be the case. Therefore, letters A, B, D and E did not replace arrows numbered 1, 2 and 8. Using the same principle, letters B, C and G could not replace arrows 2, 3, or 4, letters A, C, E and H could not replace arrows 4, 5, or 6, and letters A, C, D, F and H could not replace arrows 6, 7 or 8. Also, letter C could not replace arrow 5 as this would return you to the square containing one dot, as would the letter H if it had replaced arrow number 7. Given the above information you only have to refer to the grid to work out which arrows were replaced by the letters D and F.

A42   Who's Who?   Q2

Smith. Statements 1 and 3 are false.

A43   Before or Not Before?   Q28

1. Titus Andronicus
2. Two Gentlemen of Verona
3. Romeo and Juliet
4. As You Like It
5. Julius Caesar
6. Merry Wives of Windsor
7. The Winter's Tale
8. Measure for Measure
9. All's Well That Ends Well
10. Timon of Athens
11. Love's Labour's Lost
12. Troilus and Cressida
13. Much Ado About Nothing
14. The Taming of the Shrew
15. The Merchant of Venice
16. Hamlet
17. Antony and Cleopatra
18. The Tempest
19. The Comedy of Errors
20. King John
21. Twelfth Night
22. Coriolanus
23. Macbeth
24. Cymbeline
25. A Midsummer Night's Dream

A44   Odd One Out   Q41

B.

Group 1. The letter J has no vertical or horizontal symmetry. The letters in group 2 are symmetrical about the horizontal axis, the letter in group 3 is symmetrical about the vertical axis and the letters in group 4 are symmetrical about the vertical and the horizontal axis.

A46 Mix Up Squared Q68

S	Q	U	A	R	E	D
R	A	E	S	D	Q	U
D	S	Q	R	A	U	E
A	D	S	E	U	R	Q
U	E	R	Q	S	D	A
E	R	D	U	Q	A	S
Q	U	A	D	E	S	R

A47 Mix Up Squarely Q89

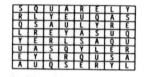

S	Q	U	A	R	E	L	Y
R	L	Y	E	U	Q	A	S
Q	S	A	U	L	Y	R	E
L	R	E	Y	A	S	U	Q
Y	E	R	L	S	A	Q	U
U	A	S	Q	Y	L	E	R
E	Y	L	R	Q	U	S	A
A	U	Q	S	E	R	Y	L

A48 Logicalympics – Swimming Q100

Event	Gold medal	Silver medal	Bronze medal
100 m freestyle	USA	GB	USSR
100 m backstroke	USA	GDR	GDR
100 m breaststroke	GB	USSR	USA
100 m butterfly	GDR	GB	GB
200 m freestyle	GDR	USA	GDR
200 m backstroke	GB	USA	USA
200 m breaststroke	USSR	GDR	GB
200 m butterfly	USSR	USSR	USSR

A49 Connection Q126
3. In each of the five rows of smaller squares, the square which is completely filled has exchanged places with one of the remaining four squares in the same row, except the fourth row from the top of the square, which remains the same.

1	2	3	4	5	6	7	8	9	10	11	12	13	14	15	16	17	18	19	20
2	18	1	6	3	13	20	14	15	12	17	11	7	19	8	10	9	16	4	5
3	20	4	12	13	16	18	15	1	9	19	10	6	17	5	8	7	2	14	11
4	3	13	14	11	12	6	5	7	8	10	9	16	15	1	2	18	19	20	17
5	15	19	11	7	18	3	9	2	17	6	16	4	10	20	14	13	1	8	12
6	8	5	17	18	4	1	3	19	16	13	15	10	12	9	20	14	11	7	2
7	10	8	18	19	1	15	2	20	13	3	14	11	6	12	17	4	5	9	16
8	14	17	5	9	20	2	12	16	19	7	13	1	11	18	4	3	15	10	6
9	11	10	19	20	15	14	16	17	3	2	4	5	7	6	18	1	8	12	13
10	4	20	8	12	19	16	6	13	18	9	3	15	5	17	1	2	14	11	7
11	1	18	10	6	17	13	7	3	20	12	2	14	8	19	15	16	4	5	9
12	5	11	20	17	14	4	13	18	2	16	1	8	9	7	19	15	10	6	3
13	17	14	9	16	2	19	1	4	7	20	8	12	18	11	5	6	3	15	10
14	13	16	15	10	9	12	11	6	5	8	7	2	1	4	3	20	17	18	19
15	16	2	1	8	7	9	10	12	11	5	6	3	4	14	13	19	20	17	18
16	19	15	7	2	3	17	4	14	6	18	5	9	20	10	11	12	13	1	8
17	12	9	3	15	5	8	18	10	4	1	19	20	13	16	6	11	7	2	14
18	6	12	2	14	8	10	19	11	1	15	20	17	3	13	7	5	9	16	4
19	9	7	13	1	11	5	20	8	14	4	17	18	16	2	12	10	6	3	15
20	7	6	16	4	10	11	17	5	15	14	18	19	2	3	9	8	12	13	1

A51 Patchy Problem Q107
Red patches = A, F, K, L, Q;
Yellow patches = B, G, H, M, R;
Blue patches = D, E, J, O;
Green patches = C, I, N, P.

A52 Square Cut Q13

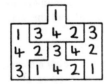

A53 Every Which Way Q23

1	2	3	4	5
4	5	1	2	3
2	3	4	5	1
5	1	2	3	4
3	4	5	1	2

1	2	3	4	5
3	4	5	1	2
5	1	2	3	4
2	3	4	5	1
4	5	1	2	3

A54 Laser Maze Q42
1. X squares = B2, B10, C10, J9;
2. Y squares = B4, C2, D4, E2, H2, H6, H9;
3. Z squares = A2, D5, I6.

A55 Coin Puzzle Q53
Place coin number 10 on top of coin number 5.

A56 Blocked Q85
Blocks rotated clockwise = A1, A3, A4, B1, B2, B4, B5, D2, E3, E5;
Blocks rotated anticlockwise = A5, C2, C3, C4, C5, D1, D3, D4, E1, E2.

A57 What Colour Next? Q93
My next-door neighbour painted his fence the following colours in the following order: Orange, Burgundy, Navy Blue, Indigo, Lavender, Olive Green, Violet, White, Turquoise, Lemon, Emerald Green, Sky Blue, Hazel Brown, Coal Black, Yellow, Mauve, Creamy White, Jade Green, Pitch Black, Fawn, Oxford Blue, Sea Blue, Purple, Primrose, Ruby Red and Red.

A58 Consider Q72
Diagram 5. All of the other diagrams consist of four shapes, each of which contains two dots. One dot is common to only the shape itself, the other dot is common to all four of the shapes.

A59 What Next? Q101
D. The pentagon contains six sections which alternate between black and white each time the pentagon rotates 72° clockwise. Five of the six sections within the pentagon have one side which is common to both the section and the pentagon. In pentagon number one, the two uppermost sections contain a black dot, as does the remaining white section. Each time the pentagon rotates 72° clockwise, all three dots rotate in an anticlockwise direction to the section which has one side common with the pentagon, two sides before the section the dot was previously in. The dots then change to the opposite colour of the section they are in.

A60 Logic Box Q122

D	O	E	L
J	P	F	C
I	G	K	B
M	A	H	N

A61 Clockwork Links Q138

The letters around the numbers given in brackets were rotated in the following order and direction:

(3) – 90° clockwise;
(1) – 90° clockwise;
(3) – 180°;
(4) – 90° anticlockwise;
(2) – 90° anticlockwise;
(1) – 180°;
(2) – 90° clockwise;
(4) – 180°.

From this I get:

A	O	Q	N	K
D	1	B	2	H
E	F	I	R	S
J	3	T	4	L
C	G	U	P	M

A62 Odd One Out Q145
B.

A63 Card Sharp Q3
E = C; F = A; G = D; H = B. As E did not appear in Row 2, it must be on the other side of A or C, and, as A had already been in the position where E is, C must be on the other side of E. As F did not appear in Row 2, the other side must show A or C, and, as C is on the other side to E, A must be on the other side of F. D must therefore be on the other side of G because, of the two positions remaining, D has already been in the position where H is. This leaves B on the other side of H.

A64   Logic Box   Q24

```
F D G
I A C
B H E
```

A65   The Animals Went In Which Way?   Q45

The animals went into the Ark in the following order:

1. Otters
2. Elephants
3. Beavers
4. Lions
5. Tigers
6. Rabbits
7. Ducks
8. Doves
9. Goats
10. Pigs
11. Snakes
12. Foxes
13. Badgers
14. Horses
15. Donkeys
16. Mice
17. Leopards
18. Squirrels
19. Monkeys
20. Swans
21. Chickens
22. Sheep
23. Peacocks
24. Geese
25. Penguins
26. Spiders

A66   Jack of All Trades   Q65

1. Journalist
2. Signwriter
3. Cartoonist
4. Undertaker
5. Illustrator
6. Postmaster
7. Pawnbroker
8. Upholsterer
9. Ringmaster
10. Newscaster
11. Programmer
12. Fishmonger
13. Chargehand
14. Blacksmith
15. Escapologist
16. Greengrocer
17. Piano-tuner
18. Lumberjack
19. Woodcarver
20. Interpreter
21. Compositor
22. Taxi-driver
23. Roadsweeper
24. Electrician
25. Gamekeeper
26. Scene-shifter

A67   Logic Box   Q81

```
B D H
I C E
G F A
```

A68 Roll the Die Q97
Three.

A69 Sparky Q111

Time	Job	Number of house
9.00 a.m.	Mend vacuum cleaner	27
10.00 a.m.	Mend dishwasher	51
11.00 a.m.	Mend fridge motor	52
12.00 noon	Install cooker point	14
2.00 p.m.	Install light in alcove	9
3.00 p.m.	Mend electric shower	13
4.00 p.m.	Mend broken socket	31
5.00 p.m.	Install wall lights	43

A70 The Host Q127
J was the host.

A71 Grid Fill – Numbers Q147
The numbers can also be fitted into the grid in a mirror image
(diagonally) of the solution shown below.

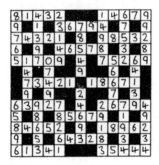

A72 Every Which Way Q5

1	2	3	4
3	4	1	2
4	3	2	1
2	1	4	3

1	2	3	4
4	3	2	1
2	1	4	3
3	4	1	2

125

A73 Number Fill Q20

5	3	7	9	4	1
9	1	8	2	8	3
2	4	3	6	4	6
5	8	7	5	1	7
9	1	2	9	2	6
5	8	7	6	4	3

A74 Number Pyramid Q35
A = 8; B = 6; C = 9; D = 7; E = 3; F = 9. The pyramid contains the numbers one to nine as follows: one 1, two 2s, three 3s, four 4s, five 5s, six 6s, seven 7s, eight 8s and nine 9s. When complete, no two adjoining rectangles contain the same number.

A75 Number Fill Q52

4	7	9	5	6	1
8	2	1	2	7	3
4	5	6	5	8	4
7	2	9	2	1	3
8	1	6	5	8	4
9	7	9	3	6	3

A76 Blocked Q66
Blocks rotated anticlockwise = A1, C1, D3, E2.
Blocks rotated clockwise = B1, B2, D1, D4, E5.
Blocks rotated 180° = A5, B3, C3, D5.

A77 Connection Q87
5. The large square contains 16 smaller squares which have been grouped into four squares of four, each group forming another square, and have been rotated clockwise or anticlockwise about the centre of each group. The upper left and lower right groups have been rotated clockwise, the upper right and lower left groups have been rotated anticlockwise.

A78 Square Cut Q96

M	C	K	E	M	K	I	J
I	I	O	E	L	B	G	G
N	K	J	E	H	B	H	L
P	B	G	A	A	D	P	E
F	J	B	A	A	D	N	G
F	N	D	I	F	D	O	N
P	F	H	C	O	L	C	P
O	M	H	C	L	J	K	M

A79 Odd One Out Q113
C.

A80 Logic Cube Q128

TOP LAYER: BACK

J	S	A
Z	K	I
B	W	L

FRONT

MIDDLE LAYER: BACK

C	M	T
Q	G	X
N	U	D

FRONT

BOTTOM LAYER   BACK

E	P	H
V	@	Y
O	F	R

FRONT

A81 Laser Maze Q142
1. X squares = C1, E8, F3, F4, F8, H3, H9, I9;
2. Y squares = B6, E3, H2, H5, I3, I6, J4;
3. Z squares = A6, B3, B9, C6, E1.

A82   Odd Ones Out   Q27

Cubes numbered 2, 5 and 7 cannot be formed from the flattened cube shown.

A83   Laser Maze   Q7

1. X squares = A9, D8, E4, G10, J2;
2. Y squares = C2, C4, F8, G8, H6, I7;
3. Z squares = A4, E2, I2.

A84   Monarch E   Q40

The solution is historically correct. The years which the monarchs reigned over England are included in the solution below.

Egbert	827 to	839
Ethelwulf	839	858
Ethelbald	858	860
Ethelbert	860	865
Ethelred	865	871
Edward the Elder	899	924
Edmund	939	946
Edred	946	955
Edwig	955	959
Edgar	959	975
Edward the Martyr	975	978
Ethelred the Unready	978	1016
Edmund Ironside	1016	1016
Edward the Confessor	1042	1066
Edward I (35 years)	1272	1307
Edward II (20 years)	1307	1327 (Deposed)
Edward III (10 years)	1327	1377
Edward IV (22 years)	1461	1483
Edward V (1 year)	1483	1483
Edward VI (6 years)	1547	1553
Elizabeth I	1558	1603
Edward VII (9 years)	1901	1910
Edward VIII (abdicated)	1936	1936
Elizabeth II	1952 to date.	

A85 Age Old Question Q58

1. Harry	9. Martin	19. Philip
2. Leonard	10. George	20. Michael
3. Bill	11. Simon	21. John
4. Jimmy	12. Ian	22. Keith
5. Tom	13. Colin	23. Barry
6. Eddie	14. Arthur	24. Robert
7. Kevin	15. Paul	25. Dave
8. Fred	16. Matthew	26. Joe
	17. Neil	
	18. Frank	

A86 Square Cut Q73

A87 Wordsquares Q83

1. MADE	2. MANE	3. OMEN	4. DAME
AMEN	AREA	MORE	AGED
DEMO	NEAR	ERNE	MERE
ENOW	EARN	NEED	EDEN

A88 Number Fill Q98

1	9	15	11	8	3	8	12
6	14	5	1	6	2	5	6
12	11		11	12		8	12
1	7	5	7	14	2	7	6
13	9	2	1	8	3	9	13
10	4		11	15		7	10
13	3	5	14	2	3	9	13
10	4	15	4	15	4	14	10

A89 Post Problem Q105

A90 Nine by Four Q117

	A	B	C	D	E	F
1	9	7	4	2	9	3
2	3	8	6	1	6	8
3	9	2	4	3	5	1
4	1	6	1	7	2	7
5	8	4	2	4	6	3
6	9	5	8	5	7	5

A91 Combination Q132

K, H, B, C, E, A, D, F, G, I, J.

A92 Housing Problem Q143

1 = L	7 = P	13 = G
2 = D	8 = I	14 = E
3 = K	9 = A	15 = O
4 = Q	10 = M	16 = F
5 = B	11 = C	17 = H
6 = J	12 = N	

A93 Stationary Stationery Q8

George carried the three small parcels. Fred carried the two medium-sized parcels. Arthur carried the large parcel.

A94 Grid Fill Q25

A95 Colour Cube Q34

The smaller cubes can form a larger cube as described if placed in the following positions:

Top layer

23	26	10
17	6	3
1	12	22

Centre layer

18	25	2
4	19	21
14	11	8

Bottom layer

15	27	13
24	5	16
20	7	9

The colours of the faces of the above cube are:
1 Looking down on the cube – Yellow.
2 Looking from beneath the cube – Violet.
3 The remaining faces are as shown below:

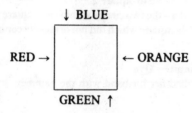

A96 People's Pets Q44

George Anderson lives in Chestnut Crescent and he has a pet budgie called Percy. The full solution is as follows:

1. Tom Williams owns the fish called Fred and lives in Maple Grove.
2. John Thompson owns the dog called Benson and lives in Cedar Road.
3. Bill Smith owns the rabbit called Rodney and lives in Pine Avenue.
4. George Anderson owns the budgie called Percy and lives in Chestnut Crescent.
5. Harry Hudson owns the cat called Spike and lives in Willow Street.

```
I C E
D G A
H B F
```

A98   Connection   Q63
2. If the squares are numbered 1 to 9 as if reading conventionally, the following changes occur:

Square 1 – contents move to square 3.
Square 2 – they move to square 1.
Square 3 – they move to square 2.
Square 4 – they move to square 5.
Square 5 – they move to square 6.
Square 6 – they move to square 4.
Squares 7, 8 and 9 – the two circles within each square move to the two corners of the square which did not originally contain a circle.

A99   Whodunnit?   Q74
Lady Logic killed her husband with the hammer.

A100   Odd Block Out   Q79
Number 3 is the odd one out as all of the others are different views of the same block.

A101   Coin Puzzle   Q94
Form a square with three coins on each side, then place another coin on top of each corner coin.

A102 Logic Box   Q103

F	O	D	N
G	B	I	C
H	J	A	K
E	M	P	L

A103 Odd Block Out   Q114
Number 8 is the odd one out as all of the others are different views of the same block.

A104 Odd One Out   Q123
A.

A105 Odd One Out   Q133
B.

A106 Logic Cube   Q140

TOP LAYER: BACK

K	Y	A
Q	T	D
J	V	N

FRONT

MIDDLE LAYER: BACK

0	S	G
P	B	W
C	H	U

FRONT

BOTTOM LAYER: BACK

X	E	O
M	F	I
R	Z	L

FRONT

133

A107 Flipover Q6
The letters were flipped over the numbers shown in brackets in the following direction:

(1) – vertically;
(2) – horizontally;
(3) – horizontally;
(4) – vertically.

A108 Done What? Q19
Dave did it. If only one person is telling the truth and Charlie didn't do it, then it must be Charlie who is telling the truth as he said that he didn't do it. Therefore all of the other statements must be false. Dave said that Bill did it which isn't true, Bill said that Arthur did it which isn't true and Arthur said that Eddie did it which also isn't true. The only person remaining who could have done it is Dave.

A109 Flipover Q36
The letters were flipped over the numbers shown in brackets in the following order and direction:

(2) – vertically;
(1) – horizontally;
(2) – vertically;
(3) – horizontally;
(4) – vertically;
(3) – horizontally.

A110 Logicalympics – 100 Metres Q50

Race	1st	2nd	3rd	4th	5th
1	A	B	C	D	E
2	D	E	A	B	C
3	B	C	D	E	A
4	E	A	B	C	D
5	C	D	E	A	B

AIII Piano Lessons   Q67

	MORNING		AFTERNOON	
	NAME	GRADE	NAME	GRADE
MONDAY	BRIAN	ONE	JOHN	THREE
TUESDAY	SUSAN	TWO	BRIAN	ONE
WEDNESDAY	JILL	FIVE	LUCY	FOUR
THURSDAY	TOMMY	ONE	JULIE	THREE
FRIDAY	LUCY	FOUR	SUSAN	TWO

AII2 Sweet Tooth   Q77
Tracey – toffee;
Alan – chocolate-covered mints;
James – plain mints;
Robert – mint-flavoured toffee;
Neil – chocolate.

AII3 Odd One Out   Q102
Number 8. All of the others remain the same if flipped over about the vertical, horizontal or any of the two main diagonal axes.

AII4 What Next?   Q116
Six
Three
Five
There is one word between the two 'ones', two words between the two 'twos', three words between the two 'threes', etc.

AII5 Mix Up 16   Q129

1	2	3	4	5	6	7	8	9	10	11	12	13	14	15	16
2	6	9	13	1	5	10	14	8	4	15	11	7	3	16	12
3	9	12	2	14	8	5	15	11	1	4	10	6	16	13	7
4	13	2	15	10	7	12	5	6	11	8	9	16	1	14	3
5	1	14	10	6	2	13	9	3	7	12	16	4	8	11	15
6	5	8	7	2	1	4	3	14	13	16	15	10	9	12	11
7	10	5	12	13	4	15	2	1	16	3	14	11	6	9	8
8	14	15	5	9	3	2	12	16	6	7	13	1	11	10	4
9	8	11	6	3	14	1	16	15	2	13	4	5	12	7	10
10	4	1	11	7	13	16	6	2	12	9	3	15	5	8	14
11	15	4	8	12	16	3	7	13	9	6	2	14	10	5	1
12	11	10	9	16	15	14	13	4	3	2	1	8	7	6	5
13	7	6	16	4	10	11	1	5	15	14	8	12	2	3	9
14	3	16	1	8	9	6	11	12	5	10	7	2	15	4	13
15	16	13	14	11	12	9	10	7	8	5	6	3	4	1	2
16	12	7	3	15	11	8	4	10	14	1	5	9	13	2	6

A116 Logic Cube Q134

TOP LAYER: BACK

Z	G	D
U	W	O
A	J	N

FRONT

MIDDLE LAYER: BACK

P	V	C
J	K	O
F	X	B

FRONT

BOTTOM LAYER: BACK

R	Y	H
L	E	@
M	S	I

FRONT

A117 Temple Teaser Q141

The order of the statues, from right to left, is as follows: Moirai, Ate, Nike, Rhea, Nemesis, Hebe, Pleiades, Iris, Chloris, Hygiea, Opis, Terpsichore, Amphitrite, Artemis, Eos, Tyche, Danae, Hestia, Selene, Hera, Athene, Persephone, Irene, Aphrodite, Hecate, Demeter.

A118 Letter Boxes Q9

D	E	F	H	I	J	C	G	B	A
F	C	G	A	J	E	H	D	I	B
E	B	A	I	C	D	G	J	H	F
B	D	H	C	E	G	I	A	F	J
I	J	E	G	B	H	F	C	A	D
A	G	C	B	D	I	E	F	J	H
C	H	B	J	G	F	A	I	D	E
J	F	I	E	H	A	D	B	C	G
G	I	D	F	A	B	J	H	E	C
H	A	J	D	F	C	B	E	G	I

A119 Flipover Q22
The letters were flipped over the numbers shown in brackets in the following order and direction:

(3) – horizontally;
(2) – vertically;
(1) – horizontally;
(2) – horizontally;
(3) – vertically;
(4) – horizontally.

A120 Connection Q38
5. There are four stages in the connection between the squares.

1. All three columns of squares are overlapped and combined to form the column on the left of the connecting square.

2. The resulting figure in the top square of the left-hand column is then duplicated into the bottom square of the centre column and the centre square of the right-hand column.

3. The resulting figure in the centre square of the left-hand column is then duplicated into the top square of the centre column and the bottom square of the right-hand column.

4. The resulting figure in the bottom square of the left-hand column is then duplicated into the centre square of the centre column and the top square of the right-hand column.

A121 Uncle Christmas Q51
Uncle George will get the scarf for Christmas. (Uncle Raymond will get the gloves, Uncle Victor the hat and Uncle John the tie.)

A122 Logic Box Q69

A123 Boxed Q82

Left   Right

Box colour:	Red	Yellow	Green	Blue
Glove colour:	Green	Blue	Red	Yellow
Scarf colour:	Blue	Red	Yellow	Green

A124 Clockwork Links Q104

The letters around the numbers given in brackets were rotated in the following order and direction:

(1) – 90° clockwise;
(2) – 90° clockwise;
(4) – 180°;
(3) – 180°;
(4) – 90° clockwise;
(2) – 180°;
(1) – 90° anticlockwise;
(3) – 90° anticlockwise.

A125 Logic Box Q115

A126 Advanced Academics Q130

ALWIN	ANSON	ABNER	ANTON	ALWYN
ABDUL	ATHOL	ALVES	ABRAM	ALBAN
AUBYN	AIRAY	ARIEL	ALBAT	AMAND
ALGIE	ANGUS	AARON	ALLAN	ARCHY
ANDRE	ALROY	ASKEW	AUREL	ALRED

A127 Whodunnit? Q144

The butler killed Lady Logic in the kitchen using the knife.

A128   What Next?   Q11

The next most appropriate square is C.

Each square is divided into four smaller squares. All four of which contain two changes each time the sequence progresses.

1. TOP LEFT-HAND SQUARE: The dot moves from corner to corner of the square in an anticlockwise direction and the 'T' lines rotate 45° in a clockwise direction.

2. TOP RIGHT-HAND SQUARE: The dot moves from corner to corner of the square in a clockwise direction and the straight line rotates 45° in an anticlockwise direction.

3. BOTTOM LEFT-HAND SQUARE: The dot moves from corner to corner of the square in an anticlockwise direction and the straight line rotates 45° in a clockwise direction.

4. BOTTOM RIGHT-HAND SQUARE: The dot moves from corner to corner of the square in a clockwise direction and the 'T' lines rotate 45° in an anticlockwise direction.

A129   The History of Invention   Q17

Invention	Year
Gunpowder	1320
The telescope	1607
Pianoforte	1710
The mercury thermometer	1721
The spinning jenny	1763
The steam engine	1764
The hot air balloon	1783
The miner's safety lamp	1815
The sewing machine	1841
Steel	1856
Dynamite	1868
The telephone	1876
The phonograph	1877
The wireless	1898
The tank	1899
Radar	1935
The jet engine	1939
Polyester	1941

A130   Done What?   Q32
Charlie did it.

A131   All the Twos   Q43
1. Eric and Alex.
2. Frank and Doug.
The results of the two races are as follows:

Race	One	Two
1st	Eric	Colin
2nd	Alex	Brad
3rd	Colin	Eric
4th	Brad	Alex
5th	Frank	Frank
6th	Doug	Doug

A132   Done What?   Q62
Harry did it.

A133   Odd One Out   Q80
C.

A134   Grid Fill   Q95
The words can also be fitted into the grid in a mirror image
(diagonally) of the solution shown below.

A135 Say Cheese Q109
From left to right: Cheddar, Edam, Tilsiter, Pecorino, Port Salut, Parmesan, Jarlsberg, Roquefort, Cheshire, Brickbat, Swiss, Cotswold, Lymeswold, Camembert, Gorgonzola, Wensleydale, Gouda, Brie, Gruyère, Gloucester, Cottage, Gambozola, Stilton, Mycella, Boursin, Westminster Blue.

A136 Clockwork Links Q124
The letters around the numbers given in brackets were rotated in the following order and direction:

(1) – 90° clockwise;
(2) – 90° anticlockwise;
(4) – 180°;
(2) – 90° clockwise;
(4) – 180°;
(3) – 90° clockwise;
(1) – 180°;
(3) – 90° anticlockwise.

A137 Blocked Q136
Blocks rotated clockwise = A3, A4, B2, B5, C2, C3, C4, C5, D1, D5, E3, E4, E5;
Blocks rotated anticlockwise = A1, A2, A5, B1, B3, B4, C1, D2, D3, D4, E1, E2.

A138 Blocked Q12
Blocks rotated anticlockwise = A2, B1, B2, C3, C4, D3, D5;
Blocks rotated clockwise = A4, B5, D1, D3, E1, E4.

A139 Safecracker Q64
4 2 1 3 is the correct combination.

A140 Somewhere Q79
Do you live here? If you are in village A the answer will be yes. If you are in village B the answer will be no. It does not matter if the resident is actually from the village or not, the answer would still be the same.

A141 Odd Block Out Q47

Number 6 is the odd block out. All the others are different views of the same block.

A142 Connection Q106

5. Each of the 25 small squares contain a cross, or, a circle. In the connecting square, all of the crosses of the original square have been deleted, as have the circles which were in the centre of a diagonal, vertical, or horizontal line of three squares, with the two other squares in the line containing a cross.

A143 Wordsquare Q14

P	L	A	T	E
L	I	N	E	N
A	N	E	N	T
T	E	N	S	E
E	N	T	E	R

A144 Clockwork Q54

The letters around the numbers given in brackets were rotated in the following order and direction:

(2) – 90° anticlockwise;
(4) – 180°;
(3) – 90° clockwise;
(1) – 180°;
(2) – 90° clockwise;
(3) – 180°;
(4) – 90° anticlockwise.

The first two rotations could be the other way round, i.e. (4) – 180° and then (2) – 90° anticlockwise, as there is no further effect on either until the letters around the number (3) are rotated.

B	E	D	A	I	F	H	C	J	G
C	I	E	D	G	A	J	F	H	B
G	C	J	F	H	D	I	A	B	E
I	H	B	C	A	J	E	G	D	F
A	J	I	E	B	C	G	D	F	H
E	A	F	J	D	B	C	H	G	I
D	B	A	G	C	H	F	E	I	J
J	F	H	B	E	G	D	I	C	A
H	G	C	I	F	E	B	J	A	D
F	D	G	H	J	I	A	B	E	C

A	B	D	F	C	G	E	I	J	H
F	H	J	D	E	A	I	G	C	B
H	I	B	G	J	E	C	F	D	A
E	A	C	I	G	F	D	B	H	J
J	F	E	C	D	B	A	H	G	I
D	G	F	B	A	J	H	C	I	E
C	D	A	J	I	H	F	E	B	G
B	J	I	E	H	D	G	A	F	C
I	E	G	H	B	C	J	D	A	F
G	C	H	A	F	I	B	J	E	D

G	I	C	F	A	D	B	J	H	E
E	C	B	A	I	F	J	D	G	H
C	G	A	H	F	E	D	I	J	B
D	E	F	G	H	J	A	B	C	I
J	H	I	D	G	B	E	C	A	F
A	D	H	B	J	G	F	E	I	C
F	J	G	E	D	C	I	H	B	A
H	F	D	C	B	I	G	A	E	J
I	B	E	J	C	A	H	G	F	D
B	A	J	I	E	H	C	F	D	G

A148 Where Do They Live? Q21

1 – Brown;
2 – Johnson
3 – Anderson;
4 – Krishnan;
5 – Singh.

A149 Blocked Q49

Blocks rotated clockwise = A1, B5, C2, D4, E1;
Blocks rotated anticlockwise = A4, B3, C3, D2, E5;
Blocks rotated 180° = A3, B1, C4, D5, E2.

A150 Connection Q16

4. (The square has been flipped over about the horizontal axis.)

□